SOME REFLECTIONS ON
JURISPRUDENCE

SOME REFLECTIONS ON
JURISPRUDENCE

BY

W. W. BUCKLAND

Archon Books
1974

Library of Congress Cataloging in Publication Data

Buckland, William Warwick, 1859-1946.
    Some reflections on jurisprudence.

        Reprint of the 1949 ed. published by University Press,
Cambridge.
        1. Jurisprudence.   2. Law—Philosophy.   I. Title.
Law   340.1   73-13713
ISBN 0-208-01407-1

First published 1945
Reprinted 1974 with permission of Cambridge University Press
in an unaltered and unabridged edition as an
Archon Book, an imprint of
The Shoe String Press, Inc.
Hamden, Connecticut 06514

Printed in the United States of America

Contents

Preface

This little book contains the substance of a course of lectures delivered by me several years ago, with some expansion and some additional discussions, an origin which accounts for, though it may not excuse, a certain amount of repetition. My hearers were warned that a good deal of what I had to say was heterodox and would probably be repudiated by authoritative teachers of jurisprudence, and the readers of this book are entitled to the same warning. But, whether the opinions expressed in the following pages are sound or not, it may be claimed that they suggest points of view which are worthy of consideration, of more consideration than they have hitherto received.

The title of the book is a misnomer from the analytical standpoint. Only the latter part of it is concerned with the analysis of legal concepts, the subject which Austin regarded himself as professing. Most of it deals with the prolegomena of analytical Jurisprudence, that is, with the meaning of the word 'law' as the subject-matter of Jurisprudence. Though 'law' is the material of Jurisprudence, 'law' is no more a legal concept than courage is a courageous concept. The word Jurisprudence is wide enough to cover this. Thus there is some trespassing into the Philosophy of Law, but only a few prominent legal philosophies are discussed, only such as make contact with Positive Law, and only in so far as they make this contact.[1]

I have to thank my friends, Dr C. K. Allen, Dr D. Daube, Professor Lauterpacht and Sir Arnold McNair for reading the

[1] I regret that Dr Friedmann's excellent *Legal Theory* reached me too late to be utilised in the text.

typescript and making very valuable criticisms and suggestions. But it is more than usually necessary to say that this does not imply their acceptance of all or any of the views expressed by the writer.

I have also to thank the proprietors of the *Cambridge Law Journal* and the *Law Quarterly Review* for permission to utilise matter which has appeared in their pages, and the officers of the University Press for their unfailing care and helpfulness.

W. W. B.

I

Jurisprudence and Legal Philosophy

IF we look at the papers, say, on the law of contract, set in different law schools we shall see differences in emphasis and we may think some papers better designed than others, but we shall have no doubt but that the papers are set on the same subject. It is very different with Jurisprudence. We shall find the papers set in various schools so unlike that we shall be inclined to doubt whether the different examiners are dealing with the same subject. And, in fact, they are not. 'Jurisprudence' is a most hospitable word. It can be understood to include not only the analysis of legal concepts, which is what Austin meant by it, but also all those topics which are discussed under the rubric 'Philosophy of Law'. Writers on this subject may be said to fall into two groups.

(*a*) Those concerned with the rational basis of law, those who attempt to discover the reason why law is binding on us and what, if any, are the limits on the binding force of law. This may be said to concern lawyers, for if there are limits on the binding force of law the lawyer ought to know about them. They have the further interest that some of these writers have the habit, as we shall see later on, of treating rules which cannot be squared with their views as to the rational basis of law as not law at all. With this point of view they tend to overlap with

(*b*) Those (e.g. Kant) who seek to formulate an ideal system of law, wholly independent of any actual system. To this group belong writers on the 'law of nature'. This seems to be no more in effect than an intuitionist system of ethics, confined, indeed, to those duties which organised society ought, in the opinion of the writer, to enforce on its members. What a man ought to do and what he ought to be made to do are not the same thing.

With the law of nature we shall have to deal later; here it is enough to say that on one, perhaps the most usual, view of it, it is a canon to which the law ought to conform (whether in any particular case it does or does not). With this may obviously be associated the 'science of legislation' (Bentham, *Principles of Morals and Legislation*, p. 324, calls it 'Censorial Jurisprudence'), in simpler language 'law reform', which in the hands of Bentham and his followers is a system of Utilitarian ethics, with the same limitation, to what ought to be compelled.[1]

All this is very different from the 'Jurisprudence' which was Austin's real subject. This was the analysis of legal concepts. That is what Jurisprudence meant for the student in the days of my youth. In fact it meant Austin. He was a religion; to-day he seems to be regarded rather as a disease. He cannot be replaced on his pedestal; the intensely individualistic habit of mind of his day is out of fashion. But it is well to do him justice. Jurisprudence as he conceived it was merely the analysis of legal concepts. It certainly was not a philosophy of law (see Oakeshott, *Politica*, 1938, pp. 103 *sqq*.). It is true that at the very beginning of his work he describes it as the 'Philosophy of Positive Law', but he does not mean by philosophy at all what Mr Oakeshott means by it. When he wrote, the word was commonly used to mean any ordered body of knowledge or supposed knowledge (as it is in the expression 'natural philosophy') and that is all that he means by it. His business is the analysis of legal conceptions, ostensibly as they are to be found in various systems of law, actually as he saw them in English Law, with a little, not very profound, comparison with Roman Law. That is why he came to be called an 'analytical' jurist. Here there is a point to be noted. The theory of law and sovereignty seems nowadays

---

[1] Stammler (*Die Lehre von dem richtigen Recht*, 1926, p. 91) says that the questions for the philosophy of law are three. What is law? How does it come to be binding? What principles should guide the legislator? Neither of the last two is within Austin's conception of Jurisprudence, though on each of them he has something to say.

to be thought the most interesting part of his work; it is, in fact, the only part which people read. This leads to a tendency (see Professor Allen in the first essay in his *Legal Duties*) to treat the theory of law and sovereignty, the imperative theory, as the basis of Austin's claim to be an analytical jurist. But in fact this is not part of his real subject at all. Law and sovereignty are not legal conceptions; they are presuppositions. If we look at the book itself and not at modern restatements, we shall see that very clearly. It is the prolegomena to Jurisprudence. Austin called it *The Province of Jurisprudence determined* and he published it as a separate book.[1] It is an exposition of the notions about which we must clear our minds before embarking on Jurisprudence itself. We can see how he set to work. He had, as has been said, to construct the science which he was to profess. His subject being the analysis of law, he had to determine the various meanings of that word and to make clear the sense with which he was concerned, what he called 'positive law'. Of this he reached the definition 'General Command of the Sovereign'. Incidentally he had to shew what he meant by 'general', by 'command', and finally what he meant by 'Sovereign', which last notion he defined to his own satisfaction though perhaps not to everyone's. For though he claims universality for his conceptions it was long ago made clear that this claim was unfounded.[2]

1 Kelsen, 'The Pure Theory of Law and Analytical Jurisprudence (*Harvard Law Rev.* 1941, p. 54), says that 'the first edition' (*sc.* of Austin's *Lectures on Jurisprudence*) 'was published in 1832 under the name of *The Province of Jurisprudence determined*'. But, as the title shews, it was not a first edition of the Lectures, but a preliminary chapter. Incidentally, Kelsen calls the work *Lectures on General Jurisprudence*, but, as published, the title does not contain the word 'General'.

2 It is clear that the Austinian Sovereign does not exist in all States. The fact that in the United States there is no standing body or group of bodies which can make what law it likes is causing impatience in juristic and political thinking, as is noted by Brown (*The Austinian Theory of Law*, p. 163), who thinks it likely to be circumvented. As evidence of public feeling he quotes Professor Burgess. From his long quotation from this writer we may select the following purple patch. 'From the standpoint

Over large parts of the past his propositions were not true anywhere. Over much of the world they are not true now. To get out of his statements what is good we must take him with limitations which he would not have accepted, but, subject to which, he was telling the truth. What he really had in mind was contemporary English Law and primarily an English criminal statute. It is not of course maintained that Austin's is the 'true' or 'real' or 'correct' definition of law. It is obvious that a legal philosophy, a study which takes into account all stages in the evolution of law, all aspects of law (including its goodness or badness) and all rules of conduct which commonly go by the name of law (law of nations, law of nature) will need a much wider definition. All that is contended is that, for the purpose in hand, the analysis of the concepts of developed systems of 'municipal' law in the western world, including the Roman, 'prescribed by an uncommanded commander' fits the facts. It

of political science I regard this legal power of the legislature of a single commonwealth' (i.e. State in the Union) 'to resist successfully the will of the Sovereign as unnatural and erroneous. It furnishes the temptation for the powers back of the Constitution to reappear in revolutionary organisation and solve the question by power which bids defiance to a solution according to law....From this point of view all the great reasons of political science and of jurisprudence would justify the adoption of a new law of amendment by the general course of amendment now existing, without the attachment of the exception, and, in dealing with the great questions of public law, we must not, as Mirabeau finely expresses it, lose the *grande morale* in the *petite morale*.' He means that it is a bad state of things and likely to lead to trouble. He rightly recognises that to change the Constitution in a way which it does not admit is revolution and not a political act at all. He seeks to avoid this by 'interpreting' the Constitution by leaving out a clause (he calls it an exception) which safeguards State rights. This too is revolution as Mirabeau well knew. Burgess recognises the illegality, but holds it justified by Jurisprudence, by which he must apparently mean a morality, not a science of positive law. This is the same writer, who, alone among American publicists, held that Belgium, by resisting the German invasion in the last war, abandoned her neutrality and thus the action of Germany was entirely proper (see *Law Quart. Rev.* 1917, p. 99). For Burgess as for Germans the *grande morale* is the convenience of powerful communities.

serves well enough for that, but to use it for any other purpose is to invite disaster. A druggist instructs his new half-trained dispenser that he is not to make up any prescriptions containing poisons, but to leave them for his employer. He adds, 'As you may not always know what is a poison, you must note that the poisons on these shelves are the substances in blue bottles.' That is enough for the purpose, but if the apprentice applies the same principle elsewhere, there will be trouble.

II

Current Philosophies of Law and Positive Law

THOUGH the philosophies of law which we have mentioned have, strictly, nothing to do with the analysis of legal conceptions, their exponents use language which tends to obscure this fact. It will be well to pass in review some of the best known among them, dealing only with their relation to positive law: a detailed study of them is impossible in the space available and is not necessary for present purposes.

Duguit,[1] in works of which the best known in this country is that translated by Professor Laski under the title *Law in the Modern State*, wrote primarily of France, but laid down doctrines conceived as universal. For him there is no sovereignty. The basis of public law is public service. This is no longer, he says, an *a priori* formula, but has become the expression of the existing situation (p. 32 of translation). The further consequences of his doctrines are set out and criticised by Brown (*Law Quart. Rev.* 1916, pp. 168 *sqq.*), who summarises them as follows. 'The organs or agencies of Government are justified by the ends they serve. They possess a power, but the justification and the extent of that power must be determined by reference to the public services which are to be performed.... The acts that they do, if we are to be guided by precedent... are valid in so far as they promote the great ends for which they exist', and 'The [orthodox] theory affirms that statutory law as an expression of sovereign power cannot be questioned in the courts. The contrary is true in America and promises soon to be true in France.' Duguit's views, as expressions of legal conceptions, and this they profess to be, have been rejected on what seem good grounds, by,

1 For Duguit's legal philosophy, see now Friedmann, *Legal Theory*, pp. 159 *sqq.*

inter alios, Brown, cited above, and Esmein in the later editions of his *Droit Constitutionnel*,[1] but something must be said of them. He shews, clearly enough, that there are communities in which a statute made by the authority with the highest statute-making power is not necessarily valid, and thus shews that there need not be in any community such a supreme legislative power. No one nowadays would disagree with this. Duguit admits (p. 84) that the supremacy of Parliament cannot be disputed in England, and his conclusion is that there is no difficulty in conceiving a supreme legislature with limited powers and that things are tending that way. There is nothing startling in this (though not everyone would agree with the concluding proposition), but the language used is misleading. Professor Laski says (*Introd.* p. xliii), 'We recognise that the governing classes retain power, but they retain power to-day not by virtue of the rights they possess but of the duties they must perform. Their power therefore is limited by the degree in which these duties are fulfilled,' and (*ibid.*) 'Its' (i.e. the ruling class) 'acts have neither force *nor legal value*[2] save as they contribute to this end.' Duguit says (p. 39): 'They' (i.e. the elements of the idea of public service) 'consist essentially in the existence of a legal obligation of the rulers in a given country, that is to say, of those who in fact possess power, to ensure without interruption the fulfilment of certain tasks.' Here the language is that of legal obligation. In fact the writer seems, as Brown notes, not to be clear whether he is talking law or political morality. It is true that Mr Gupta (*Law Quart. Rev.* 1917, pp. 154 *sqq.*) seeks to defend Duguit from Brown's criticism. He says that Jurisprudence is an infant science, that, like those of other sciences, its theoretical principles are gradually worked out by experience and that it is futile to prescribe to a science the way it shall follow. But what is in question is not the progress and direction of progress of a science

1 See, e.g., Esmein, *Droit Constitutionnel Français* (ed. 8, by Nézard), I, pp. 46 *sqq.*
2 Italics mine.

but a confusion of language and, as it seems, of thought, in the work of a certain writer. Law and political morality are different things and it is desirable to eliminate confused writing in scientific work. No doubt the ends for which law exists are important. No doubt the study of these ends may be called a kind of Jurisprudence—Bentham called it 'Censorial Jurisprudence'—but Brown was not disputing this. What he said, and said rightly, was that analysis of law as an existing institution is one thing and criticism of it is another and that confusion results from neglect of this distinction. This neglect led Blackstone (in one passage, but not always),[1] Spencer and Duguit to say, wrongly, that a bad law is invalid. It seems to have led T. H. Green to say, wrongly, that Czarist Russia was not a State.[2] It is not very clear in what sense Jurisprudence is an infant science, but in any case it is not too young to be taught to tell the truth. Professor Laski is much too clearsighted not to see the distinction and he makes the rather grudgingly expressed remark (Introd. *cit.* p. xxv) that while the criticism of Duguit 'has legal validity it is, in sober fact, politically worthless'. What does this mean? If statements are incorrect, the pointing out of this ought to be of some value even in political morality. It is in fact an admission that Duguit's propositions are not statements of law, as they purport to be, or even of politics as an analytical science, but of an ideal political morality. It is true that there is a tendency nowadays to see governments as servants, not as masters, which may be desirable, provided we are clear that they are servants of an ideal, not of a capricious electorate. But that does not justify the language of Duguit.

Duguit held that the orthodox theory that statutory expressions of sovereign will cannot be disputed in the Courts is not true in the United States and bids fair not to be true in France (*op. cit.* pp. 83 *sqq.*). For France it is impossible to say what will happen—many strange things have occurred there since Duguit wrote—but his views were energetically denied by Esmein. In

[1] *Post*, p. 34.   [2] *Post*, pp. 34 *sq.*

fact Duguit seems to be confusing the 'sovereign' and the executive and the jurisdiction of the Conseil d'État. For the United States the proposition is quite unjustified. It is true that there is in the community no legislative body whose enactments cannot be called into question in the Courts. This, however, shews only that Acts of Congress or of other legislative bodies are not expressions of the sovereign will. They are expressions of a will which is not sovereign. There is in the Constitution a provision that no one is to be deprived of property, liberty or life without due process of law. What this meant when it was first introduced into the Constitution we need not enquire: it has been interpreted as a wide moral principle—the Constitution has many such. The effect is that any enactment of Congress or of State legislature is liable to be called into question before the Supreme Court and declared unconstitutional. That is, there is no sovereign legislature. The written Constitution is the only unquestionable authority and the Supreme Court interprets it. This is, in effect, a provision under which public policy, i.e. current morality (or rather the morality of the Supreme Court), controls legislation, just as, with us, it is used to some extent for controlling contracts. And, as with us, this 'police power', as it has been called, has been very uncertain in its operation. Professor Laski says (*op. cit.* p. xxii) that 'its main tendency in recent years has been to defeat the progress of exactly the type of measure upon the desirability of which M. Duguit would probably himself lay the gravest emphasis'.[1] This shews that the opinions of the Supreme Court, in the field in which they can make their views effective, do not agree with those of Duguit. There would be more disastrous differences if Duguit's principles were really in operation.

It should be remarked that if, as in the United States, a written Constitution can control the legislature, there is no reason why such limits should not be introduced into other Constitutions, even unwritten Constitutions. The result would be that there would be no sovereign legislature. If, in a given case, the House

[1] See, for illustrations, Friedmann, *op. cit.* pp. 53 *sqq.*

of Lords decided that the legislature cannot possibly have meant what it clearly did mean, because it was contrary to natural justice, or the social purpose, or what not, and Parliament took no steps, a doctrine might grow that an Act of Parliament might be held void in the Courts as being contrary to public policy, etc. Such a doctrine could arise if, and only if, powerful opinion was in favour of it. But this is not in point. The question is not whether it could happen but whether it has happened. It does not appear to have happened. What Duguit shews is that communities may exist in which there is no sovereign legislature and that the fact that a rule is in statutory form does not necessarily prove that it is valid in law. No one will dispute these propositions, but they are useless for his purpose. They do not in the least shew that as a matter of law (and this is what the passages above cited claim) legislation is controlled by 'social purpose'.

It is an essential part of Duguit's theory, indeed it is its basis, that enactment and decision (*jurisprudence* in the French sense of the word) do not really make law. All they do is to discover or at most formulate it (*op. cit.* ch. 3). They may create subsidiary rules—he calls them 'constructive laws'—to give effect to the 'formative laws', but these they merely find. According to him, what creates these is not natural justice or any ideal, but the common consciousness, what the mass of opinion regards as fit to be law.[1] It is this view which leads him to the conclusion that anything enacted inconsistent with the 'social purpose', of which mass opinion is the test, is not law at all. Of course he gives only a narrow field to these 'formative laws'. In France he finds only three: respect for property, freedom of contract and no liability without fault. He allows to legislation and doctrine great influence in forming mass opinion, so that a statute which in his view was not law when it was enacted may come to be law by conversion of mass opinion. All this has been effectively criticised. This 'mass opinion' is totally indeterminate. If a statute is passed as to which public opinion is evenly divided, what is

[1] This is much like Krabbe's *Rechtsgefuehl, post,* pp. 13 *sqq.*

the law? Do the French Courts, when a formally enacted statute is presented to them for application in a case, refuse to apply it because they do not think it agrees with mass opinion? Not one of his three 'formative laws' is accepted anywhere without serious restrictions. If decisions or statutes are to guide this mass opinion, not merely to follow it, they must presumably be acting on some norm. What is this norm? Since, by the hypothesis, it is not public opinion as to what is right, it must be some light specially vouchsafed to the legislature and the Courts. It seems to be natural law disguised, and it is natural law made, as by Blackstone (sometimes) [1] and Spencer, the test of the validity of the law and not merely an ideal. The 'formative laws' are without meaning apart from the applications which are made by the 'constructive' rules, and since, where the legislature is supreme, the Courts enforce the enacted law, whatever it is, the formative principles are without the enforceability which is essential to anything which the lawyer can call law.

It will be seen that Duguit set out to find a rational basis for law (though he cannot be said to succeed), and, supposing himself to have done so, tries to shew that what does not satisfy his test is not law at all, that is, tries to find a legal reason for disregarding what men call the law, where he disapproves it. Something of the same sort is to be found in the work of Dabin (*Philosophie de l'ordre juridique positif*) of the Catholic University of Louvain, who writes under the aegis and the control of the Church of Rome. For him the enquiry into the rational basis of law is in the moral field, quite outside the juristic. He finds this moral basis in the law of nature, which, for him, is a moral intuition. The law of nature provides only a few broad principles which are, however, for him, authoritatively elaborated by the Church—*la Morale Chrétienne*. He admits that a rule of law, whether it conforms to these principles or not, is law and is enforced by the State, but it is only where it does so conform that there is a moral duty to obey it. Not every one will admit

[1] *Post*, p. 34.

the moral intuition which he affirms and only members of his
Church will accept the authoritative elaboration. But, allowing
for this, and for the fact, which he hardly takes sufficiently into
account, that, independently of the merits of a law, disobedience
to law is itself an evil, since it tends to break up society, there
is little to quarrel with, so far, in his thesis, from a legal point
of view. But in his detail there seems to be confusion between
the legal and the moral. He tells us (p. 4) that 'droit', the 'droit
des juristes', consists of rules enforced by the State; its characteristic is compulsion and he tells us that, whenever he speaks
of 'droit' simply, that is what he means. Later on he defines
this 'droit' (p. 34) as laid down and sanctioned by the public
authority. So far so good, but he adds 'en vue de réaliser dans
les rapports humains...l'ordre le plus favorable au bien commun'.
If this is to be taken literally, as it stands, it follows that a rule
not framed with a view of realising the order most favourable
to the common good is not law at all. The inference is that if a
given law aims at the common good, it is law, but if it does not
achieve its aim there is no moral obligation to obey it. If, however, it does not even aim at the common good, it is not law at
all; it is not even legally binding. No lawyer would accept this.
Towards the end of his book, when he is discussing unjust laws
(p. 724) he says 'il est un devoir antérieur à celui-là' (respect
for law)...'c'est le devoir qui incombe aux gouvernants de ne
proposer à l'obéissance des citoyens que des lois justes ou con-
formes à la justice (*sensu lato*). Si l'on admet que le pouvoir des
gouvernants n'est pas arbitraire, qu'il est, au contraire, fonctionnel
et donc essentiellement limité, il est impossible de ne pas aboutir
à la conclusion que, de soi, la loi injuste n'a pas la vertu d'obliger.'
No doubt he means 'd'obliger moralement', but he leaves us in
the dark as to the meaning of 'essentiellement limité'. His language is astonishingly like Duguit's, though he is often at pains
to express his rejection of Duguit's theories (see pp. 642 *sqq.*,
716). Another point in his discussion is significant. Before giving
his definition of (juristic) law he tells us that he is going to analyse

it (p. 34). He indeed does so at length, but, to the surprise of the reader, there is nowhere any discussion of the last part of the definition, i.e. of the requirement that the law must aim at the public good. Since it purports to be a definition of the actual law, a rule which does not aim at the public good cannot be even legally binding. This, as we saw, is inconsistent with what he says elsewhere. In the hands of a Catholic jurist, this may not be dangerous, for he accepts an authority which tells him what is an unjust law. But in the absence of such an authority, since one man's opinion as to what aims at the public good is equal to any other man's, it seems very like anarchy. In any case his doctrine is inconsistent with itself. These different views all seeking and finding a rational basis for law, i.e. a good reason why the law is binding on us, tend, Duguit's most definitely, to the view, inadmissible in fact, that any rule which does not conform to the excogitated basis is not law at all.

Krabbe (*Die Moderne Staatsidee*, ed. 2),[1] also seeking a rational basis for law, leaves us in a little doubt whether a law which does not conform to this principle is really a law or not, whether indeed there can be a law which does not satisfy it. His rather mystical doctrines are not easy to state in a few words, but an attempt must be made to do this (see, especially, chh. 1-3). From the old notion that the State creates the law thought has already passed to the *Rechtsstaat* in which it is the law which creates the State. The State is based on the law. But it is necessary to go further. State and law are really identical; they are both merely expressions of the real power which is not vested in the law or in the State, but in the idea of law, *Rechtsgefuehl*, present in man. We do not find the sovereignty notion in Greece, where Plato's *Nomoi* shews that power was thought of as belonging not to persons but to ideas. The conception of sovereignty served in its time a useful purpose, but among western races it is not really now admitted and ought therefore to pass out of the teaching of

1 English translation by Sabine and Shepard, *The Modern Idea of the State*.

the theory of the State. Personal power has been replaced by impersonal; instead of *sic volo, sic iubeo* we have now a *geistige Herrschaft*, an impersonal control. It follows that *geltendes Recht*, the really valid, is that which is rooted in the *Rechtsgefuehl* or *Rechtsbewusstsein* of men. It is the representative system which has brought about the change. In this system a norm gets its bindingness not from any external 'source' but from the spiritual life of man, to be found in his *Rechtsgefuehl*. Every man has this *Rechtsgefuehl*, feeling for law, just as he has for morals, aesthetics and so on. It may be rudimentary, a mere *Rechtsinstinkt*, or it may be highly developed, a *Rechtsbewusstsein*, and this *Rechtsbewusstsein* operates as an obligatory force. The view that attributes the force of the law to sovereignty is not tenable. It is impossible to deny power to ideas; as everyone knows they have caused revolutions and changed Constitutions. However, this *Rechtsbewusstsein*, in which the power really rests, applies only to those interests which affect the people and of which they can have some understanding. The *Rechtsbewusstsein* of individuals is not all alike, but tends to become so by experience and living in association. If it does not, the society falls to pieces. There can be no contradiction in the law—there must be unity of the norm. The majority principle gives this. The view of the majority has the highest value. Though one *Rechtsbewusstsein* differs from another in quality, this does not mean that they are not based on a common legal sense (*Gerechtigkeit*) but that in different persons there are, in different degrees, disturbing factors. More important is the difference in knowledge of the interests concerned. Only those should have lawmaking entrusted to them, on certain interests, who have by experience knowledge of those interests—there should be much more decentralisation than there actually is.

It is to be noted that in all this Krabbe is not talking of ideals, of might-have-beens, but of the law of the land and the question what it is which makes it binding on us. There seem to be four fundamental points in his doctrine. The power is in the principles of law itself. The State and its organs are only the form in which this power expresses itself. The law, the real law, is that which accords with the *Rechtsbewusstsein* of the people subject to it. The majority has an innate capacity for being right, in law. It is difficult for the plain man, or at least for one plain man, to understand these doctrines.

There is, no doubt, a sense in which most great historical events have been 'caused' by ideas. In that sense the ideas of Rousseau made the French Revolution. But it was the man Rousseau who made these ideas effective by communicating them.[1] Till he did so the ideas were inert. It was other men who gave them a distorted expression in the 'red fool-fury of the Seine'. The proposition means only that men are inspired by ideas. It is untrue to say that in any sense material to political discussion *Macht* lies in the hands of ideas. It is incorrect to say, as Krabbe does, that this principle governed the Greek world and to treat Plato's *Nomoi*, the expression of a philosopher's view of the ideal law, as if it were an expression of the Greek legal system. His illustrations give a test of his doctrine. He says that his view is already that of the legal systems of Western Europe, its triumph having been assured by the introduction of the representative system. It must follow that this is the state of things in England. This cannot be reconciled with the fact that a formally passed Act of Parliament cannot be challenged. It will not do to say, as Krabbe perhaps would, that Parliament is the voice of the authoritative *Recht*. What assures us of this? If there is an authority behind which we cannot go, which in fact enforces its commands, it seems absurd to say that it has no power. One cannot say that it is a delegated power, for the abstract *Recht* cannot do any act, even of delegation. If we invoke the notion of determinism, we must say that neither Parliament nor *Recht* nor anything else has any power. If we say that it is conclusively presumed to express *Recht*, this is a mere dogmatic postulate and cannot be

1 Ideas, says Sir Ernest Barker, possess a dynamic force 'when once they have been enunciated in a form of authority' (Foreword to Oakeshott, *Social and Political Doctrines of Contemporary Europe*, p. vii).

the basis of a rational theory. Krabbe, however, seems to rest his view on the proposition that a majority has the magical power of always being right, or, rather, of expressing *Recht*, however it contradicts itself. Its opinion has the 'highest' value. We may leave him to make his peace with Ibsen's Dr Stockmann (cited by Dr Allen, *Democracy and the Individual*, p. 42) who said, 'The majority is never right.'[1] In any case it is a mere dogma and a most untruthlike one. Krabbe might say that Parliament is the expression of the *Rechtsgefuehl* of the nation. So far as this adds anything, it leaves the same dilemma. Either Parliament is supreme or there is some power within the Constitution which can override it. It may be that Krabbe (like Duguit speaking of the State) tends rather to confuse the supreme legislative power and the executive. But he is speaking of the law and it is from that point of view that we are considering his views. It may be that a sovereignty cannot give a rational justification of its existence. That historical facts have put it into a position of supremacy is, in itself, no justification. But that is a question not of law, though it ought to interest lawyers, but of political philosophy. The lawyer has to face facts; if he does not, as Austin says, the hangman will in the last resort demonstrate the weakness of his argument. It is an uneasy recognition of this fact that has led to the rise in Germany of a school of writers who demand that judges should be entitled to free judgement, not, at least as to some of them, being bound by *Gesetz*, but only by *Recht,* of which presumably they are to be the judges. In a world of good men this might work very well, but in the world as it is this would be 'Cadi justice' and a denial of law. Krabbe says that to require fixity in law is an error, as conditions are always changing. That is true; law is not unchangeable. But what civilisation needs is a reasonable certainty of law and continuity in its administration, and neither of these will be provided by such Cadi justice.

Krabbe maintains—it is his central point—that we have a *Rechtsgefuehl* which can be refined into a *Rechtsbewusstsein,*

[1] He had been anticipated by Schiller and others.

analogous to the moral sense, *Sittengefuehl*, and that this tells us what is *Recht*. It is true that he does not trust it far. It applies only to interests which affect the people and which they can understand, and it is to be trusted only where the persons expressing it have some knowledge of the matter. That amounts to the reasonable view that the making of law on a point should be in the hands of those who know something of the matter. It is more or less what happens with us. The majority votes the law, but its preparation has usually been the work of experts. And the judges who, from time to time, make new laws are also experts. But it does not justify the view that the supreme legislature expresses the *Rechtsgefuehl* of the people and so gives us *Recht*. Krabbe uses the majority rule as a way out of the difficulty. He tells us that the majority opinion has the highest claim to represent the nation, that it is in some way sacrosanct. He treats what is in fact a rather clumsy way, used for lack of a better, of finding out what legislation is desirable, as having some necessary infallibility about it. His view ignores the facts that in all but strictly party measures a part of the majority on one Bill or clause may be in the minority on another so that the infallibility of its decision depends not on any qualities of its own but on the actions of other people, and that the majority carrying the Bill may be far from representing the majority of the people concerned. He does not, however, hold that the majority is always right, but only that it expresses what the *Rechtsgefuehl* of the majority thinks right: that is *Recht*. Thus he reaches the view that, at any rate in a democracy, all the law is valid and legally binding (thus differing from the writers already mentioned). In practice we know that it is valid and legally binding. But this does not give us a rational basis for this bindingness, and it is not provided by Krabbe's dogma that there is something sacrosanct about the vote of a majority. What we want and do not get is a reason why the will of the majority should bind the minority.

Is this alleged *Rechtsgefuehl* anything but an illusion? A *Sittengefuehl*, a moral intuition, is intelligible, though there mare any who deny its infallibility and others who deny its existence. But a *Rechtsgefuehl* is a very different matter. To determine what kinds of duties the law should enforce, at what point it should intervene and how it should intervene, these are not matters to be solved by intuition; they call for wide experience, a knowledge of the world.[1] There is no problem more important than that of a just law; there is no problem more difficult. Stammler (*Lehre von dem richtigen Rechte, cit.* p. 111) speaks contemptuously of *Rechtsgefuehl*. He says that to treat this as a source of *Recht* is trusting to a mystical something which remains in the background. A general notion that society needs law may indeed be admitted. A negative sense, a notion of the duties which law cannot be expected to enforce, is possible but doubtful, for opinions on this result from exact reasoning. When we consider how complex is a modern political society, how difficult are the problems which present themselves to the most specially trained minds as to what is or what ought to be the law in a given situation, it is impossible to believe in this natural sense for law or that all legislation which emerges from Parliament exactly represents the electorate's *Rechtsgefuehl*. All Krabbe depends on this, but even accepting it we have got no rational basis for law.

Krabbe's doctrine that the real power (*Macht*) is in the idea, the law, and that the agencies which we see are merely carrying out its behests is tantamount to saying that the State and the law are one. Another view seeking a rational basis for law and reconciling this with the validity of all actual law is that of Kelsen, who develops the 'pure theory of law'. Kelsen's writings are voluminous and not easy reading, but his main doctrines have been made more accessible to English readers by Professor Lauterpacht's account of them in the collection *Modern Theories of Law*, 1933, pp. 105 *sqq.*, by articles written by Kelsen (translated by Mr C. H. Wilson) and published in the *Law Quarterly*

1 As Ihering says (*Zweck im Recht*, 1, Pref.), it is not *Rechtsgefuehl* which makes law, but law which makes *Rechtsgefuehl*.

Review, 1934, pp. 474 *sqq.*, 1935, pp. 517 *sqq.*, and an article by Mr Wilson, in *Politica*, 1934, pp. 54 *sqq.*[1]

His main doctrines are two:

I. He holds, like Krabbe, but more categorically and more consistently, that the State is not a man or group but a system of norms; the State is a system of norms coterminous with the law. The juridical order looked at as a system of restraints is the law, looked at as a system of norms it is the State. But Kelsen does not, like Krabbe, vest power in the State so conceived; he holds, rightly, that power is in the hands of living beings. Thus for him there is no will of the State; all wills are wills of living men. It is very difficult to pin down writers to a definition of the State, but here we have one which is at least precise. Since all activities of the State may be said to be making or applying law, it may be thought that we need not go behind that. We can make State mean law, if we wish, but we must bear in mind that we now mean by State something other than most men mean by the word. It is not merely a different definition; it is a definition of a different thing. For most people the State is an entity which does things. The law does nothing. It is people who exercise activities, not norms. In his *Law and Peace in International Relations* Kelsen brings out (p. 65) the fact that the State, as a system of norms, does not act: all State acts are done by individuals. It is difficult to realise the relation of these individuals to a system of norms. Are they its agents or organs? Can a system of norms have agents or organs? An agent is authorised by somebody. An organ is set in motion by somebody's will. But a system of norms cannot authorise and has no will. It seems more reasonable to say that the State is a number of people (though it may not be easy to say what people (*post*, pp. 73 *sqq.*)), if we use the word State at all, rather than Sovereign, and that it is this body which gives orders, i.e., legislates. Indeed, in 'The Pure Theory of Law and Analytical Jurisprudence' he says (*Harvard Law Review*, 1941, p. 51), 'Norms by which indi-

1 See also Friedmann, *op. cit.* pp. 99 *sqq.*

viduals are obligated or empowered issue only from the law-creating authority'. That authority is for him, as the context shews, the State. But the State which acts is a number of people. We may think of the State as a group of persons enforcing norms and so producing effects in the external world (though there are wide differences of opinion as to the constituents of this group) or we may think of it abstractly as a Power. In either case it does things. We may say that it does them through its organs or agents, but a set of norms cannot have agents or organs. It took a philosopher of the calibre of Mr Bumble to credit the law with at least mental activities. 'If the law supposes that, the law is a ass—a idiot.' When we read Professor Lauterpacht's sympathetic account of Kelsen's theories we come on what looks at first like an inconsistency, for he speaks repeatedly of 'persons who form part of the State', and men can hardly be parts of a system of norms. But there is no inconsistency, since, for Kelsen, a 'person' in law is not a human being but a set of norms (*Law Quart. Rev.* 1934, p. 496). It is difficult to apply the notion to the possible case of a dictator ruling purely by caprice, issuing what Austin calls 'particular commands'. In such a community there would be no law, but if it was stable and orderly it is difficult to say there is no State.

This part of Kelsen's doctrine is less important for our present purpose than the other.

II.   That part of Kelsen's doctrine which has been set out above gives us his view as to the nature of law, the kind of phenomenon it is. The bald account of it here given, sufficient for the present purpose, does not of course do justice to the wealth of learning or to the acute reasoning to be found in Kelsen's writings. He is not concerned with the merits of the law, with the goodness or badness of any specific rules contained in the law. He is dealing, as he tells us, with the pure concept of law, and all other matters are irrelevant. Nor has he, so far as we have gone, been concerned with the rational basis of law, the reasons why the law is binding on citizens. The second part of his theory deals with this point. Every specific rule of law, he says, owes its validity to the fact that it is an application of a wider, superior rule. In any system of law, the widest or highest is the Constitution. This he treats as the summit or basis (it is the same thing) of the legal system. Since every rule rests on this Constitution, he then faces the question: What gives the Constitution this validity? His answer is that we must assume a superior rule, an ideal or hypothetical super-Constitution, and he disclaims any theory of natural law. This hypothetical superior norm cannot be juristic, and the question arises how it, in turn, comes to be binding. As it stands it is very much in the air. We cannot think of it as similar in kind to the hypotheses set up by workers in the physical sciences, for these are constantly tested by experiment and rejected if they prove not to work, but it is obviously impossible to submit this assumed super-Constitution to any tests at all. And it is impossible to think of it as axiomatic, as a proposition which, though it is not susceptible of proof, is what is called obvious to common sense. It is, on the contrary, a notion at which common sense, unless some evidence for it is given, must inevitably protest. Having supposed a super-norm we may indeed suppose another still superior norm, and so on *ad infinitum*, like the elephants and tortoise which have been supposed to support the earth. Clearly there is no help in that. It is not surprising that the disciples of Kelsen sought for another basis. They found one by a remarkable inversion of ordinary notions. An appeal was made to natural law, but a natural law of very little content: its only precept is *pacta sunt servanda*. International law arose by agreement and owes its validity to this principle. International law in its turn has recognised State law, which owes its validity to this recognition.[1] Thus the superior norm is a precept of international law to the effect that there may be States and their laws are valid. The original theory, leaving the super-norm in the air, was in one respect better than this second stage, which is a Social Contract theory with the nations

1 See Schiffer, *Die Lehre vom Primat des Völkerrechts.*

as parties instead of the members of a civil community. It is better in that it is not demonstrably a fiction, only there is no sort of reason to believe it. The super-Constitution is a non-jural postulate. The lawyer is quite entitled to say that he does not look beyond this, that he accepts the bindingness of the law as a datum. But neither he nor the philosopher is entitled to say that it explains the binding force of law. An arbitrary postulate proves nothing. The second theory, with its authorisation of State law by international law, is a plain fiction. It seems doubtful whether there was any international law in ancient times, whether in fact States admitted any rights in other States except as the result of agreement, and whether breach of such an agreement was not regarded rather as an offence against their own gods than as a breach of duty to the other State. But, however this may be (and there are differences of opinion), there seem to be difficulties about this authorisation. In the expression international law 'nation' must mean 'State'. And though there may be an unsolved question of priority between the chicken and the egg, it will probably be agreed that the individual came before the herd, that there must have been a State before there was a group of States. But if there was a State there was law, since, for this school of thought, law and State are the same thing. What were these communities, which must have been organised, since they seem to have sent delegates to a convention? In truth there never was such a convention. There never was such a recognition. The thing is imaginary.

It might indeed be argued (not however by Kelsen himself, since he wholly repudiates natural law) that international law, being a law of nature, exists independently of the existence of States. But a law of nature to the effect that all Constitutions of whatever kind are valid is difficult to accept, and nothing else will serve.

Supporters of the Social Contract could put into it any terms they pleased, and we know that it has been interpreted in different ways, e.g., by Hobbes and Locke. And *ius naturale* has

different contents in different minds. Even those who confine it to the rule *pacta sunt servanda* can excogitate cases to which the rule would not apply. But this super-norm, to which the actual Constitution owes its validity, must, it seems, conform to the existing Constitution; it is a god made in man's image. It follows from it that every rule of law is binding. Kelsen does not seem to call his super-norm a moral or rational principle; it just exists.

The theory has undergone many changes, especially at the hands of Verdross.[1] The changes do not seem to affect the main structure and we cannot pursue them here. But it may be noted that an appeal is made to Article 38 (3) of the Statute of the Permanent Court of International Justice, which includes among the sources of law the 'general principles of law recognised by civilised States'. This seems to supersede the maxim *pacta sunt servanda* if indeed it does not absorb it, for most people would expect to find this maxim among the 'general principles of law'. This is no more satisfactory. If it means 'positive law', then the law seems to be its own basis, for principles of positive law presuppose positive law. This does not appear convincing. If it means law in a wide sense, it seems to be indistinguishable from natural law. It means the opinion held by most reasonable thinking men that there ought to be law enforced by the 'State', that this law ought in general to be obeyed and that certain rules ought to find a place in it, though as to the identity of these rules there would be wide differences of opinion. But this again does not provide a basis, a rational process which compels us to regard the positive law as binding.

All these things, Krabbe's *Rechtsgefuehl*, Kelsen's super-norm, the Social Contract and the rest, are alike. They are all ingenious imaginings which do no more than disguise the fact that the writers have not found any ultimate reason why law should be regarded as binding. Of course, in any investigation, if we are trying to reach ultimate truths, we commonly reach a point at which we

1 Carefully set forth and examined by Schiffer, *op. cit.* pp. 224–49.

can get no further back and have to rely on some axiom or postulate which cannot be proved. And the conceptions which we have been considering are sometimes regarded as such postulates. But they are very different in nature from those with which we meet in, e.g., Euclidean geometry. These latter are propositions which cannot indeed be proved, but, in the three-dimensional Euclidean world in which the ordinary man lives, are confirmed by his experience. They may not be absolutely true, but they are at least truthlike. He knows, or believes with a good deal of empirical justification, that he can rely on them. He cannot help believing in them. But this super-norm, the law-creating *Rechtsgefuehl*, the Social Contract, and so forth, are of a very different character. They are not confirmed by experience. They are not truthlike. The Social Contract assumed never in fact happened. There was never an international convention conferring validity on State law. And if one cannot prove that the mysterious *Rechtsgefuehl* is an unreality, one can at least say that it is unevidenced—there is no reason to believe in it. We cannot use mathematical postulates as warrant for these others. The relation between them is not a real similarity but only a remote analogy.

The theory of Jellinek (*Allgemeine Staatslehre*), so far as the writer understands it, is not an explanation either. In his view something which he calls the State, not defined, but, as it seems, a group of persons, finds itself in possession of power, and establishes rules. These are the law. This process he calls 'auto-limitation'. It is true that a body with supreme power does make law. An autocrat, man or group, without rules, may do justice, though it probably will not, but it does not make law—there is no *Rechtsstaat*. But autolimitation is, as Professor Brierly notes (*Recueil des Cours de l'Académie de Droit International*, 1928, III, pp. 482 *sqq.*), a contradiction in terms. If the State's power is limited, it must be by some superior power. But even accepting the analysis, we are no better off. We do not know what the State is or how it came by this power, what 'right' it has to it.

It does not appear how this power, even 'autolimited' so as to be law, can constitute a rational basis for a moral duty to obey. This 'psychological' theory, as Mr Jones says (*Historical Introduction to the Theory of Law*, p. 209), 'has only helped to confirm the metaphysicians in their conviction that the first step towards a philosophy of law is to accept frankly its metaphysical implications'. This, however, is to rest it on an unproved and unprovable assumption, which has no basis in experience, or, as in the case of the Social Contract, on an historical basis which is not true.

Stammler's theories,[1] so far as the writer has seen them, are of a different character. He is not concerned with the question what it is which makes a rule law; it is immaterial whether it is the act of a Sovereign or anything else. The notion of law is an abstract conception which is a part of experience only when embodied in concrete rules. It is these rules with which he is concerned. The *richtiges Recht* which he expounds in his *Lehre von dem richtigen Recht* is not exactly an ideal law: nothing is *richtiges Recht* which is not already actual law. But some *Recht* is not *richtiges Recht*. Having established a test of what is *richtiges Recht*, by close and difficult reasoning and not by any *Rechtsgefuehl*, which he repudiates, he proceeds to examine the various branches of law, dealing mainly with the *Buergerliches Gesetzbuch*, and to consider how far they are *richtiges Recht*, and also to shew how a number of rules, when properly interpreted, do in fact lead to *richtiges Recht*. Professor Ginsberg (*Modern Theories of Law*, p. 38) quotes from Stammler the sentence: 'whoever would be a philosopher of the law must first breathe the dust of legal archives' and, as he has not done this, confines himself to the discussion of the philosophical implications of Stammler's work. As the present writer is no philosopher he will confine himself to that part of Stammler's work which has a direct bearing on the notions of positive law, the 'law of the land'. Stammler says

[1] Only Stammler's contacts with positive law are here dealt with. For his legal philosophy in general see Friedmann, *op. cit.* pp. 87 *sqq.*

(*op. cit.* p. 57) that all established law is an attempt to be *richtiges Recht*, that is, is an attempt to satisfy the requirements of what he considers the law ought to be, into which we need not go. If this were so, it would materially affect our definition of the law, for we could then properly introduce into our definition the purpose of the law. But it can be objected that there have been, or certainly may have been, governments whose rules, or some of them, did not aim at this. To this he has a twofold reply.

i.   No case will be found in which a governor has acted without any social aim at all, but only for personal ends. This is unsatisfactory. It is an historical question not to be disposed of by an assertion. Most of us have met in private life orders issued by one in authority with only personal aims, and with no regard for the limited social purpose which he ought to have in view, e.g. a father, and it is hardly possible but that such things should have happened in the political sphere. It is not a question whether the whole course of legislation was governed solely by subjective aims but whether any single rule was, and, difficult as the historical question may be, it is very optimistic to say that there is no such case. And even if every law made by a commander had some public aim, was not merely for his private ends, had always some taint of public service about it, it cannot properly be called an attempt at *richtiges Recht* unless the real aim was the public interest. If I distribute a number of loaves, some of them poisoned, in the hope of poisoning an enemy, I cannot be said to have attempted to do good because I hoped that some would get good nourishment out of my loaves. But, apart from this, there is no reason to think his proposition true.

ii.   If there are such cases, a mere personal misuse in no way removes the point necessarily aimed at (*den in der Sache notwendig gelegenen Zielpunkt*). If a quack betrays the confidence of his patient, this does not alter the fact that in the appeal to his skill, objectively considered, the aim of real knowledge is nevertheless implied. If a tyrant uses the machinery of legislation for purely subjective ends, this does not remove the objective direction of legal thought towards the right. The present writer is not sure that he understands this, but if he does, it is in no way to the point. The analogy of the quack would justify only the statements that the public usually expect to find the law laid down in the general interest and that there is usually a pretence that it is so laid down. The *Zielpunkt* in the case of the quack is present or implied only in the sense that one party believes it to be present. That is different and does not help him. The case of the tyrant, as explained, would justify only the statement that systems of law, as a whole, usually have a public interest more or less in view. This is a very different thing from the statement that *alles Recht* is an attempt at *richtiges Recht*. It is a very small matter compared with the rest of Stammler's work, but it is worth mention because the statement that every law is laid down in the public interest may easily be perverted into the statement that every law must be so laid down. Stammler would not say this, but others would. Thus Mr Parker, in his edition of Salmond's *Jurisprudence*, says (p. 62) that a so-called law which does not aim at justice is not law at all. From the correct statement that some law is not *richtiges Recht* it is easy to pass to the untrue proposition that a *Recht* which is not *richtiges Recht* is not binding. For the expression 'not binding' is ambiguous. It may mean 'is invalid at positive law', in which sense it is untrue. It may mean 'has no rational basis', which may be true, and an important matter for politics. But it is in the first sense that it is repeatedly used, as we have seen, by Duguit and others.[1]

The writers we have been discussing break, it will be seen,

---

1 Writers who base law on the 'general will' have excogitated a real will which is not the actual will. Friedmann, *op. cit.* p. 236, cites Fascist philosophers to the effect that 'the individual is real only in so far as he thinks and acts the universal' and that 'the State is not the will of the majority, it is the true, rational will of the individual, expressing itself in the community'. This world of ideas in which a man wills something which he does not will at all is one which the present writer does not venture to enter. But this law which is always aiming at being *richtiges Recht*, and is therefore binding, seems to belong to that world.

into two groups with different aims. Duguit and Dabin, dealing with bad laws, seek to find reason for refusing any moral obligation to obey a bad law, and the former consistently, and the latter incidentally, confuse the asserted absence of moral obligation with absence of legal obligation. Krabbe and Kelsen are seeking to find a rational basis for all law, good or bad, and Stammler, by holding that all law is at any rate trying to be good law, seems to be in the same camp. They are facing the real problem: Is there a rational basis for all law, an obligation, other than legal, for obedience to law? They all agree that there is, but in the foregoing pages it has been sought to shew that the bases on which they rest their conclusions are unsatisfactory. But most men feel that there are reasons, other than the fact that it is commanded, for obedience to law. These writers seem to be in error in supposing that these reasons must be of a special, often mystical, kind. *Rechtsgefuehl*, Social Contract, law of nature, super-norm— these imaginings do not help and a more pedestrian way may be better. The 'rational basis of law', i.e. the moral reasons why we should obey the law, are the same as should guide us in any other matter of conduct. It is not for the writer to determine the basis of moral obligation, a question which has agitated philosophers ever since thinking began. There is nothing here peculiar to Jurisprudence. No doubt, in applying whatever principle we adopt, the factors peculiar to law come in. The mere fact that an act is forbidden or ordered by law is important; the question is: How important? It may well be that of two courses one may seem to us the better but for the fact that the other is commanded, and that fact may turn the scale of our preference. For law is order and civilisation, and disregard of it may set an example leading to 'red ruin and the breaking up of laws'. It is an ordinary question of morals. A point may sometimes be reached at which the evil of the commanded act may be so great as to outweigh this consideration and there is no moral obligation to obey the law. No doubt, to a convinced anarchist, the fact that the act was commanded by the State would swing the pendulum the other way. The question is not settled by deciding whether the act ordered is just or unjust, assuming that we know what justice is and also assuming there is a moral obligation to justice. There is obviously a further question: Will our disobedience to this law, which we think unjust, or which is in fact unjust, lead to disregard of other laws by other people? Our conduct, so far as it goes, and so far as it is known, will in some degree encourage anarchy. Is that danger a greater or less evil than that caused by obedience in the given case? And may not our disobedience to this law breed in us a habit of disobedience to other laws which may be perfectly just though we do not like them? And may not the law have other functions than the provision of justice, which are served by the law to which we object? These questions cannot be answered by any formula. Those of Kelsen and Krabbe set out, it seems, to disprove any right to disobey any law. They are in fact no more than assertions. There may be a moral right to disobey a law, but the mere fact that a law is not just and does not serve any other purpose proper to law is not of itself enough. He would be a very bold man who attempted to lay down beforehand when the moral right of disobedience arises.

With the writers who are trying to formulate ideal systems of law, analytical Jurisprudence has, directly, little concern, for the ideal and the actual are very different things. But recent writers have expressed doctrines which ignore this and make the plain man wonder of what world the writer is discoursing. The source is a confusion between the real and the ideal, an optimistic doctrine that what the writer thinks ought to be actually is. It is assisted by another reflection, in itself sound, i.e., that there are *de facto* limits to the power of a so-called omnipotent legislator. There are laws which he would not dare to make and in the long run the course of legislation is determined by the dominant thought of the time. That is of course not a new idea. Montesquieu (*Esprit des Lois*) has a great deal about it. More than a century ago the French Academy offered a prize for an essay on 'L'influence des mœurs sur les lois'. In our own time

Dicey (*Law and Opinion in England*) and Pound (*Interpretations of Legal History*) have luminously illustrated the proposition. But this does not justify some recent utterances. If a Sovereign is deterred from certain legislation from fear of revolution, this throws no doubt on his capacity to legislate as he will, for revolution is the negation of civil society and the making of law presupposes such a society. If he refrains from legislation which he thinks desirable, not from fear of revolution, but because it is unpopular and will be evaded, this no more throws doubt on his constitutional power than would his abstention by reason of some personal interest of his own.

III

The Actual and the Ideal

No one would think of the matters last considered as having a bearing on the omnipotence of the legislator but for the inveterate confusion, already mentioned (*ante*, p. 1), between those topics with which the 'jurist' is concerned and that part of legal philosophy which Austin calls, more simply, 'Principles of Legislation', and Bentham also calls 'Censorial Jurisprudence' (*Principles of Morals and Legislation*, ch. xvii, sect. 2). The confusion is helped no doubt by Austin's old-fashioned use of the word 'philosophy' to denote any body of ordered knowledge, perpetuated in the titles of the Professorships of 'Natural Philosophy' at Oxford and Cambridge. The confusion is plain in Hastie's comment on Maine. Maine says (*Ancient Law* (Pollock's ed.), p. 136) that there is widespread dissatisfaction with current theories of Jurisprudence and a conviction that they do not really solve the problems they set out to solve. Hastie, in the preface to his translation of Kant's *Philosophy of Law* (p. xxv), says that the present unsatisfactory condition of the 'Science of Right' in this country could not be better indicated. But what Maine means by theories of Jurisprudence is theories, and not only Austin's, on the conception of positive law. What he contends for, as the context shews, is historical Jurisprudence, the attempt to come to an understanding of the conception of law by study of the circumstances of its growth, a method which he considers to have been neglected by everyone but Montesquieu. That is no doubt true; the English writers on Jurisprudence had neglected history. But what Hastie, as a follower of Kant, is contending for is quite a different study. It is the search for an ideal system of law, a search which has no relation to the analysis of an existing system of law, though it may afford a criterion of the merits of such a system. This is not what Maine is concerned with; he would have said of it, as he says elsewhere (*Early History of Institutions*, p. 370) of Austin's incursion into Utilitarian ethics, 'it is at best a discussion belonging not to the Philosophy of Law but to the Philosophy of Legislation. The jurist, properly so-called, has nothing to do with any ideal standard of law or morals.' He would have been interested in Dicey's *Law and Opinion* and in Pound's *Interpretations*, but his concern would have been, not with the rightness of the successive opinions and interpretations, but with their existence and their effect on the law. Hastie fails to distinguish between the two subjects and, by calling his book *The Science of Right*, adds to the confusion by using one of the most ambiguous words in the English language.

Kant's *Philosophy of Right* is a part of his philosophy of conduct, itself a part of his general philosophy. But to the system conceived and expounded by him and his successors any actual system is no more than, at best, an imperfect approximation. So far as these writers deal with actual law, they call it enacted or positive law and they study it only as a series of approximations to, or aberrations from, the true way, aberrations to be explained in many ways. All this is not our 'Jurisprudence'. But the narrowness and isolation of a study which aims only at analysing the conceptions of existing systems would not seem to them, any more than it does to Mr Oakeshott (*cit.*), worthy of the name of a philosophy. For it is one of the main businesses of a philosopher to find for the subject at the moment under discussion its proper relation to other subjects of thought. The legal philosopher is indeed concerned with positive law, since he must have it at command when he sets out to put his philosophy to the purpose which is the main justification for any philosophy or science, i.e. the bettering of existing conditions. What is called by Austin the 'Philosophy of Positive Law', being essentially an analysis of the conceptions of our law, is represented by, let us say, German lawyers, as a part of their statement of the law; it is the *allgemeiner Teil*. And our jurists commonly treat the philosophy or science of legislation, which is an important part of what is called by writers in other countries the philosophy of law, as being no concern of theirs. In an important sense that is quite right; much confusion has been caused by the failure to realise that it is a distinct subject. But that attitude has its dangers. It is true that this matter is no part of analytical Jurisprudence, but it should be present to the mind of every lawyer who is more than a simple practitioner, since one of his businesses is the betterment of the law.[1]

No doubt the law does set up in a sense a moral standard, and is in the main aiming at right conduct; a view of law which ignores this is misleading. But this is not a reason for including in our definition of law what is not necessarily true of the 'law' with which legal analysis is concerned. Vinogradoff says (*Common Sense in Law*, p. 42): 'Law aims at right and justice however imperfectly it may achieve this aim in particular cases....If we omitted this attribute from our definition, we should find it very difficult to draw the line between any kind of arbitrary order as to conduct, e.g. the levying of blackmail by a regular association.' Vinogradoff speaks with high authority, but it is respectfully suggested that the view here stated is mistaken. There have been wicked laws (it is enough for the argument to say there may have been) not aiming at right or justice or the benefit of the community, but inspired by private animosity. Such things were none the less laws. And the blackmail illustration ignores the point that the central authority enforces laws, but will not enforce the orders of the blackmailers, a much more manageable test than their morality. The case creates no difficulty except where the blackmailers control the State Courts, in which case their rules are the law. To leave out the notion of enforcement by the State would make the rules of a society which decided to suppress vice, by sending vicious persons 'to Coventry', actual law, for they aim at right, justice, the betterment of the community. To introduce goodness into the definition of a law is like introducing

1 See, e.g., Cardozo, *Paradoxes of Legal Science*, p. 27, quoting Cohen.

ability to trot into the definition of a horse. A horse which cannot trot is still a horse, though a bad horse. A law ignoring justice is still a law, though a bad law. It is to be noted that even Vinogradoff, in his final definition of law (p. 59), says nothing of goodness or badness. Law is 'a set of rules imposed and enforced by a society with regard to the attribution and exercise of power over persons and things'.

The notion of rightness or wrongness as being material to the validity of a law appears again in the old conception of natural law, which did good work in the development of modern international law.[1] Blackstone applied the notion to our English Law. 'The Law of Nature is binding all over the globe in all countries at all times: no human laws are of any validity if contrary to this' (Introd. to *Commentaries*, sect. 2). But he knew better and his editor cites from the same introduction (sect. 3) the words, 'If the Parliament will positively order a thing to be done which is unreasonable, I know no power in the ordinary forms of the Constitution with authority to control it'; and again, 'if we could conceive it possible for the Parliament to enact that he' (i.e. a judge) 'should try as well his own causes as those of other persons, there is no Court that has power to defeat the intentions of the legislature'; and again, 'the legislature being in truth the sovereign power is always of equal, always of absolute, authority'. This overriding law of nature, which Blackstone declared but plainly did not believe in, appears again in modern writings, though usually in a disguised form. It is as true of the law as it is of the State that it has purposes. T. H. Green, having stated what in his view is the proper purpose of the State, and therefore of its laws, i.e. the forwarding of the self-development of the people, discusses Russia under the Czars. Its practices did not conform to this principle, and he says (*Principles of Political Obligation* (ed. Bosanquet), p. 137): 'We only count Russia a

1 And elsewhere. See, for the history of theories of natural law and the part or parts that it has played, Pound, *Introduction to the Philosophy of Law*, pp. 33 *sqq.*, and Friedmann, *op. cit.* Pt. II.

state by a sort of courtesy, on the supposition that the power of the Czar, though subject to no constitutional control, is so far exercised in accordance with a recognised tradition of what the public good requires as to be on the whole a sustainer of rights.' Still more categorically he adds (p. 138) that a so-called State which does not aim at the common good is not a State at all. This is perhaps only a piece of rhetoric, rather out of place in its severely reasoned context, but on the face of it it makes the reality of a State (and thus of its laws) depend on their conformity to a standard arrived at *aliunde*.[1] That external overriding standard is essentially the law of nature, whether it is so called or not. H. Spencer, in his *The Man* versus *the State*, is really maintaining, in the chapter on 'The great political superstition', that there is no inevitable need in a legal system for an uncommanded commander. Austin would have disagreed, wrongly: it is known that there are systems which have no such figure. His further contention that it is undesirable that there should be such an uncontrolled power does not concern us. But much of his language might be used to support the contention that there is in fact no such power. There is much play with the difficult word 'right'. On p. 96 he says, 'if it is said to be "right" that

---

1 Russia was a State, and a *Rechtsstaat*, though its laws were oppressive and there was much corruption. It may be doubted whether Nazi Germany could be called a *Rechtsstaat* at all. In Germany, since 1942, the judge has been free to apply what is called the law, or not to apply it, as he thinks fit. The judge had no real independence; he was at the mercy of the executive and he would find it advisable to decide as the executive wished him to decide, irrespective of statute or precedent. It seems to have been much the same in Italy under Mussolini. A few years ago the late Professor Kantorowicz said in conversation that an Italian judge had complained that his task had recently become much more difficult. In the early days of the régime it was fairly simple. In any litigation the decision had to be in favour of any party to the suit who was a Fascist, but now that everybody was a Fascist it was not so easy—sometimes you had even to go into the merits. We know little of the conditions in Russia today, but the Codes seem to leave the judge such a free hand that the citizen must find it difficult to say what the law is in a given case.

they should carry them on' (i.e. life-sustaining activities) 'then, by permutation, we get the assertion that they have a right to carry them on'. 'Permutation' seems hardly the right word for this. He is using the word 'right' in two different senses. If we substitute for the first 'right' some equivalent such as 'fit and proper' the whole proposition becomes nonsense. And as he is contending that the position of the lawyers is a mere superstition, his second 'right' must mean 'legal right'. He implies that every man has a legal right to do what is morally right, which many trustees know to their cost not to be at all true. On pp. 80 *sq.* he uses language which might be the source of some extreme doctrines now current. Hobbes (*Leviathan*, ch. xv *init.*) says that apart from covenant there can be no injustice and 'therefore before the names of just and unjust can have place there must be some coercive power to compel men equally to the performance of their covenants'. Spencer (*op. cit.* p. 80) points out some of the objections to this passage and adds: 'accepting both his premises and his conclusions we have to observe two significant implications. One is that State authority as thus derived is a means to an end and has no validity save as subserving that end: if the end is not subserved, the authority, by the hypothesis, does not exist.' Here is the quite false assumption that an institution created for a certain purpose has no powers except such as subserve this purpose. This is obviously not always so: whether it is or not in any particular case is a question of fact. If I give a man a power of attorney, I shall be bound by what he does unless I can shew some much stronger objection to it than that it was not at all what I wanted. For the case in question, the powers of Parliament (and we must note that Spencer is talking of law, not laying down moral truisms), the answer is to be found not by juggling with the word 'right' but in history. It may well be that the absolute power of Parliament was never conferred but 'growed' like Topsy, but it exists and has existed for a long time. One who doubts it will get a plain answer from the judge. It is of no use to say that the judge is wrong; what he says is the final word.

All that Spencer's doctrine comes to, for the purposes of law or Jurisprudence, is that in his view the development of this absolute power was unfortunate.

The law of nature has played a great part in these discussions and confusions, but it is a conception which has undergone great variations, both as to its character and as to its content. Ulpian's view of it in the *Digest* (D. I. 1. 1. 3), adopted by Justinian (*Inst.* I. 2. *pr.*), making it cover the animal instincts, is of no value, and Bentham, who seems to make it represent those of primitive man, is really no better. In fact those rules commonly attributed to natural law are such precepts of right conduct as have approved themselves to fair-minded men. So stated, however, they bear no warrant of authority, and may be regarded as a form of intuitionist ethics. But their position is strengthened by basing them on the law of nature, i.e. by regarding them as rules or principles deducible from the nature of man, remembering that man is a part of nature. Kant is avowedly a supporter of the law of nature, and, however Hegel and Fichte formulate their doctrines, they are deduced from the principles of the universe, as they conceive it, and are thus, in fact, law of nature.

This law of nature has been very differently conceived at different times. For the Romans, who took it over from the Greek philosophers and gave it a juristic turn, it was no more than an ideal, hardly more than a rhetorical ornament. But the *ius gentium*, which was at first merely the informal part of the Law, which could be applied to *peregrini*, came to be thought of as universal and thus tended to be confused with the *ius naturale*. In the Middle Ages the fusion was complete and *ius naturale* came to be a test of the validity of law. By the time of the Reformation there was a further confusion, of the *ius gentium* with *ius inter gentes*, and thus *ius naturale* came to play an important part in the formation of modern international law. The final step was taken when, in the seventeenth century, a Chair of International Law was founded at Heidelberg and called the Chair of the Law of Nature and Nations, a title which Pufendorf, the first professor, gave to his book. Since then many writers have held it as in some way of binding authority, notwithstanding the fact that in most countries there has been a sovereign legislature. We have seen Blackstone accepting the dogma in some moods, but not in all (*ante*, p. 34). In the nineteenth century, Spencer, shewing that great philosophers have proved, so he holds, the existence of natural rights, rebukes English lawyers for not recognising their existence, forgetting that what philosophers were proving were natural moral rights and what the lawyers were denying were legal natural rights.[1] There is not much difference between Spencer and Blackstone. No doubt it might be desirable that the legislator should be bound to respect natural law, but the lawyer has to face the fact that he is not.[2]

[1] He seems to confuse the lawyer with the legislator.

[2] On modern revival of natural law theories, see Friedmann, *op. cit.*, pp. 48–62. So far as these have found expression in judicial pronouncements in this country and in the United States they do not seem to be much more than rhetoric. Most of us believe there is a right and wrong, and when a judge has made up his mind as to which of two admissible interpretations of the law agrees best with his moral judgement it lends a little further authority to his pronouncement to say that it is in accord with natural law or with natural justice (which seems to mean justice). But with this use of these expressions it is not surprising that the line between natural law as an ideal and natural law as a test of the validity of a law tends to become a little blurred. Friedmann speaks of the Supreme Court as applying a higher law and giving effect to inalienable rights. But, in fact, what they are doing is interpreting a certain document, the Constitution as amended. The view which they reject is not a lower law which they are overriding; they are declaring that it is not law at all, not in accord with the Constitution. The Judicial Committee of the Privy Council is constantly engaged in the same business. If the effects are more striking across the Atlantic, this is because the broad (we may almost say vague) propositions of the Constitution leave far more room for divergent opinions than do the specific provisions which the Judicial Committee have to interpret.

Our books provide, in another field, a similar unnecessary, indeed unjustified, theoretical interpretation of a judgement. The Taff Vale Case ([1901], A.C. 426) is often treated as having greatly modified the common law by giving a sort of corporateness to Trades Unions. But, as the judgements shew, all the Court did was to apply a very specific provision of a certain statute.

Most modern writers on natural law, Ahrens, Franck, Stahl and others, treat it as an ideal, a philosophy, competing with other philosophies, e.g. Utilitarianism. Those who accept it and do not make it clear that it is an ideal, avoid the obvious resulting difficulties by making it deal with only very broad notions, found everywhere, such as family ties, the notion of property, of binding compacts, etc. It is easy to justify these broad notions though the arguments are not conclusive for everyone, since each of these notions is, from time to time, attacked, and some forms of Socialism practically deny them all. If there are differences as to its bindingness, there are no less differences as to its content. For Ahrens it is almost a complete code. At the other extreme is, e.g., Verdross, for whom natural law contains only one precept—*pacta sunt servanda*—which is remarkable, as the Roman lawyers, while giving much effect to pacts, do not seem to have regarded them as creating any 'natural' obligation. Stammler's natural law with a changing content is essentially the same as Savigny's view that the fundamental principles which ought to guide the legislature are themselves subject to change in the course of historical evolution, though Savigny does not associate this with natural law. Morality is a question not only of latitude, but also of date. 'Natural law' is an unprovable postulate which it has been found convenient to assume as a basis of discussion. The last chapter of Vinogradoff's *Common Sense in Law* contains a brief but admirable account of the law of nature.[1]

Reinach[2] seeks to establish certain *a priori* notions, fundamental to law. But many of these, e.g. claim (*Anspruch*), promise (*Versprechen*) and obligation (*Verbindlichkeit*), have a field much wider than law. He observes, of his *a priori* notions, generally, that they may not occur in any positive system, so that they do

[1] On the history of the conception and the changes it has undergone, see Pound, *Law and Morals. The Historical View.* But in all its avatars it is essentially a system of intuitionist ethics, covering not all duties but those which, in the opinion of the exponent, the law should enforce.

[2] 'Die apriorischen Grundlagen des buergerlichen Rechtes', *Jahrb. fuer Philosophie und phaenomenologische Forschung*, 1913, pp. 685 *sqq.*

not bear on the analysis of the conceptions of positive law. On p. 801 he makes the interesting point that though a certain *a priori* concept may not appear in a given, or indeed in any, system of positive law, we must not speak of contradiction in the matter. The *a priori* notion is a *Behauptung*, a determination, a conclusion, while a legal proposition is a *Bestimmung*, a defining proposition, which may be right or wrong, but of which we cannot say that it is true or false; it is outside that category. It is not possible to speak of contradiction between two propositions which move, so to speak, in different planes. On pp. 839 *sqq.* he discusses the relation between his *apriorische Rechtslehre*, basic propositions found by immediate intuition, and the law of nature. He says that his *apriorischen Grundlagen* may be thought to be much the same as the law of nature, but he sharply distinguishes the two conceptions. To pursue this would carry us beyond the range of analytical Jurisprudence.

In this discussion we have necessarily trespassed a little on the confines of legal philosophy. That is beyond the scope of Jurisprudence in the strict and narrow sense in which Austin understood it, which accepts law as a datum and is concerned with analysing its content. Though Austin calls his work the *Philosophy of Positive Law* he is here using the word 'philosophy' in the sense of any organised body of knowledge. Elsewhere he calls it the 'science' of Jurisprudence. It is not now usually called philosophy. For Holland and Salmond it is a science. Markby calls his book *The Elements of Law* and doubts whether it is a science. Pollock's book (*A First Book of Jurisprudence*) also disclaims being a philosophy, and though the first part is general, the book as a whole expounds the principles underlying the common law, treated, however, in a thoroughly philosophic manner. Hearn (*Legal Duties and Rights*) hankers after a philosophy. He appears to base his work (p. 2) on a first principle that all men like to exercise power, and compares his view with that of abstract Political Economy, which assumes the end of man to be the creation of wealth. He does not in fact use the notion. If worked out it must lead to the conception of the legislature, Austin's Sovereign, as concerned only with exercising power as effectively as possible, as unlike any real system as the economic man is unlike any real man. He does refer to other aspects of Jurisprudence. He speaks of law as the result of surrounding conditions (p. 26) and he refers to the study of law from the point of view of its merits (p. 27), but his subject is the analysis of a legal system without reference to these other matters. For Lightwood (*The Nature of Positive Law*) and for E. C. Clark (*Practical Jurisprudence*) it is clearly a science. We will be content so to regard it and not as a very exact science. For those who see in law the command of a Sovereign and nothing more (if such persons exist), it is hardly that. The mere will of a Sovereign cannot be a science. But no one really does so think of it: there is much more in it than that, though nothing more, or very little more, is needed for the purpose of defining it, i.e. establishing its *differentia* which marks it off from other phenomena.

IV

Jurisprudence not a Philosophy

THERE is another reason why Austin's 'General Jurisprudence' cannot be called a philosophy. A philosophy would have in view the whole scheme of thought expressing the relation of the immediate subject to other concepts of the mind. 'General Jurisprudence' analyses a group of phenomena carefully isolated from everything else. The same point of terminology may arise in connection with political science. This may be concerned with the analysis and evolution of existing political systems or it may be concerned with their merits, with their approach to or departure from the ideal political society, as the writer conceives it. But though the principles which should guide a legislator constitute a subject which ought to interest a lawyer, since he is or ought to be a law reformer, and law reformers have fortunately not waited till the philosophers are agreed, it is quite distinct from our Jurisprudence. This is concerned with positive law. It defines the phenomenon, as a preliminary to getting to work upon it. It enquires how it came to be what it is, and considers the meaning and working of the main ideas contained in this law. It has so to speak both its anatomical and its physiological sides. But just as human physiology is not concerned with the construction of a perfect physical man, with organs free from the defects of our actual organs, so the physiology of law is not concerned with ideal codes. But the cases are not the same. The eye cannot be improved; the law can. A scientific student of law will note defects and consider on what principles these can be remedied. A lawyer should have this in his mind, but no advantage accrues from confusing the two subjects of study. Apart from Austin's short excursion into Utilitarianism, which is really no part of his subject, it is meaningless to say that Austin and Kant do not agree; they are dealing with different things. What Kant is discussing is an abstract law which does not exist in any community. What Austin analyses is the law which he observes in operation in certain communities.

In this country, more than in most, there is need for the lawyer to keep in mind both topics. Here more than on the continent the lawyer shares in legislation. The Courts are constantly making law.[1] For professional reasons the advocate must try to know in what direction the Court is likely to lean. This may be only worship of the jumping cat, watching the prejudices of a particular judge, but there is more behind it. Dicey shewed how opinion controls the course of legislation and what he says is applicable to judicial legislation. Judges have been advocates and are men of the world.[2] But the moral notions which guide them are not always those of the moment. Judicial opinion is conservative. The Courts exercise what, according to our prepossessions, we call a moderating or an obstructive influence. A clear illustration of this was pointed out long ago in Sir J. F. Stephen's *History of the Criminal Law* (III, pp. 209 *sqq.*), in relation to the attitude of the Courts towards legislation on trade combinations, and later events have only added another chapter to the story. But all this only shews that neither advocate nor judge can avoid dealing with the moral principles which commonly lie behind the law. It does not alter the fact that the science of Jurisprudence in our sense and the science of legislation are different things. It may be objected that if anyone contemplating a certain course of action must consider not only what has been laid down but also what, in view of current moral opinion, the judge is likely to lay down when the case is before him, the line between what is law and what ought to be, *lex lata* and *lex ferenda*, is rather blurred. Can they be kept so distinct? The answer is that of

---

1 For an admirable account of the judge as legislator see Cardozo, *The Nature of the Judicial Process*, Lect. 3.

2 See Friedmann, *op. cit.* Pt. VI, for a vivid account of the ways in which ideals have affected the administration of the law.

course a lawyer must be prepared to forecast the law that the judge is likely to lay down in view of current opinion and his own characteristics, but that is not a reference to an ideal. He must consider what law is likely to be laid down, not what ought to be. He may have a strong view of his own as to what ought to be laid down and quite a different one as to what is likely to be. The last guides him in advising his client. The former will weigh, if his views are unchanged, when he comes to the Bench. As counsel he is engaged in the art of Jurisprudence; as judge he will be exercising, when it is necessary, the art of legislation. No doubt, as counsel, he will be able to urge on the Court his view of what ought to be laid down—it is in that way that he has a share in legislation. But the ideal which he sets up has no necessary relation to the rule actually laid down. Only a certain amount of confusion results from an attempt to embody these notions in an analysis of what Holland calls the 'formal aspect of law'. It may of course be called Jurisprudence; that is a word of many meanings. The study of the effect of current opinion on law is an important part of historical Jurisprudence, and we must remember that history looks forward as well as backward. The study of the purposes of society with a view to the determination of the principles of an ideal legal system is something different from this, though it may be called Jurisprudence; it is Bentham's 'Censorial Jurisprudence'. One who sees law defined as the command of a Sovereign, and sees no further, thinks the words equivalent to 'merely the command of a Sovereign',[1] and

1 In a manuscript which I have recently seen there is a reference to 'the antiquated doctrine that law consists of the commands of the political Sovereign'. Did anybody ever hold this 'antiquated' doctrine? The law, for the purposes of modern Jurisprudence, must have the element of command. It is a *sine qua non*, but it is not the whole phenomenon. A horse must have four legs, to be a complete horse, but it does not consist of its legs. A law must (for the limited purpose stated) have command, but it does not consist of command; there is much more to it. There is of course a difference. The possession of four legs does not define a horse. Many things besides horses have four legs. Our 'command' defines a law because

is tempted to ask how the study of such a thing can be a science, and our study has often been attacked from this point of view. Mistaken as this objection is (for it is much the same attitude as that of the child who does not recognise the existence of anything beyond the electric light switch to cause the illumination), it has worried modern writers and some of them seem to have gone on the wrong road to find a reply. They justify the study on the grounds that law is the expression of a philosophy. That statement is untrue for any system of positive law such as it is their business to expound; Windscheid tried to make the law represent a philosophy, but it is respectfully submitted that the value of his work did not depend on that aspect of it. One way of getting out of the difficulty is to say that there are, indeed, in the system, laws not expressing this philosophy, and therefore bad laws, but that the general body of the law does express it. The bad law is a mere monstrosity, like the fifth leg of a calf. But these laws are functional, which the calf's fifth leg is not, and there are in any system too many of them to be disposed of in that way. Thus the asserted philosophy ought not to appear in the definition of the law, though it might find a place in a popular exposition of the general nature of the system. It is incorrect, even here, for it may be doubted whether there is any system of law which, in its main lines, was framed in view of any of these philosophies. Each system has been produced by many causes, and the miracle of coincidence with the philosophy of any writer is not in the least likely to have happened. None of the philosophies can give a rational account of the opposing points of view represented in any system.

The value of the scientific study of legal principle is not this.

it is its *differentia*. It enables us to identify it. And why 'political' Sovereign? Austin speaks only of Sovereign and means simply the uncommanded commander. Others speak of the legal Sovereign, meaning the same thing. The political Sovereign may be, and is with us, not the legal Sovereign, the law maker, but the body with which in the long run political power rests, i.e. the electorate. Only in the rare case of a country which makes its law by plebiscites is the political Sovereign the law maker.

The intelligent study of any rule of law involves study of many things other than the words of the statute or decision, or opinion, in which the rule is stated. It requires study of the conditions which produced the rule, and those which have from time to time led to modification of it, and those conditions will include, *inter alia*, the 'philosophies', that is, the current views of political morality which have led to variations. It also includes study of present conditions and moralities which, if the rule comes before the Courts, will widen or narrow the construction put upon it. Add to this comparison with other systems and no one will say that there is not here material for observation, for exact reasoning and profound thought. It is hard to see what more is wanted for a scientific study. The minds, habits and emotions of men are a part of nature and the law of a country is as much a natural product as are its fauna and flora. But the 'jurisprudent's' results cannot be so precise as those of the biologist; the facts he has to deal with are more difficult to come by and to interpret. He cannot make or control the experiments; he can only watch them. Many biologists are not concerned with the origins of life; for them the phenomenon of life, as for most lawyers the phenomenon of law, is a datum on which they work.

The question, however, is otiose. The word 'science' can be used more or less widely. It seems reasonable to give the name to any subject-matter involving close reasoning and systematic thought, as law does. But there are many writers and speakers who would confine the word to mathematics and the inductive physical sciences. Others would confine it to mathematics, and Hobbes says (*Leviathan*, pt. I, ch. 4) that geometry is 'the only science which it has pleased God hitherto to bestow on mankind'. No one can say that any one of these views is more right than any other.

These grounds for considering Jurisprudence a truly scientific study are far from exhausting the matter; they are those considerations which appear most plainly to a non-lawyer. Every lawyer knows the difficulties and interest of the problems which arise within the law itself, which we need not consider. They may be said to centre on the ever-varying and incalculable 'fact', for which no statute, with whatever care, imagination and foresight it is drafted, can ever fully provide, of which no judgement, however cautiously worded, can ever take complete account. Thus the lawyer has a sufficiently difficult task even though he dispenses with a philosophy of his own. This is not to say that he ought not to have one. There have been great lawyers whom no one would accuse of having a philosophy; there have been small lawyers overburdened with their philosophies. But a man will be a better lawyer, as he will be a better architect or physician, if his mind is open to the movements of thought on the profounder issues of life, beyond his immediate professional concerns. And if his mind is so open, he can hardly fail to have some sort of philosophy of his own.

V

The Command Theory and its Rivals

AUSTIN's propositions come to this. There is in every community (but he does not really look beyond our community) a person or body which can enact what it will and is under no superior in this matter. That person or body he calls the Sovereign. The general rules which the Sovereign lays down are the law. This, at first sight, looks like circular reasoning. Law is law since it is made by the Sovereign. The Sovereign is Sovereign because he makes the law. But this is not circular reasoning; it is not reasoning at all. It is definition. Sovereign and law have much the same relation as centre and circumference. Neither term means anything without the other. In general what Austin says is true for us to-day, though some hold that it might be better to substitute 'enforced' for 'commanded'. Austin is diffuse and repetitive and there is here and there, or seems to be, a certain, not very important, confusion of thought. But, with the limitation that it is not universally true, there is not much to quarrel with in Austin's doctrine. No doubt it does not tell us very much and the main point is in no way new, but with the limitation mentioned it seems sound enough. Whether it is 'General Jurisprudence' is another matter. The 'uncommanded commander' is, however, a little unpopular. In the belief, apparently, that Austin was attempting to give, not a definition, but a picture, of law, critics have urged that there is much more to a law than the will of a legislator. Austin would not have denied this. He would have agreed that the law is an outcome of many causes and that in the long run it expresses a morality, though with many inconsistencies. That does not mean a moral code of conduct but a set of rules as to what the legislator thinks it desirable that people should be made to do—a very different matter. It is tempting to add 'in the interests of society' or the like. But that is an error; a law is a law even though it is not in the interests of society and was never meant to be. That can be no part of the conception of law; an evil law is none the less a law.

The notion of law as a command and merely a command cannot be satisfactory to anyone. That it is a command the modern lawyer has to agree. The English lawyer cannot go behind it. He and the Court are bound by an Act of Parliament. He may not even submit evidence outside the Act, as to what was really meant, not even Hansard, a rule which does not exist in continental Europe. What Parliament said is law, not what it may have meant. He cannot contend that the law is no longer binding, as conditions have changed and the evil no longer exists, or that Parliament had no business to make such a law. He cannot apply the strange doctrine, already considered, that a bad law is not a law at all. But he knows very well that law is much more than a command. The command is not fortuitous; it has traceable causes behind it. It is the outcome of innumerable causes and conditions, such as Dicey and Pound have discussed, currents of opinion and philosophies. Not every writer on Jurisprudence gives much attention to these, but Sir F. Pollock took due account of them.

Apart from these fundamental difficulties there are some minor objections to the notion of law as a command, of which something must be said.

1.   There is, it is said, no element of command in such a rule as that a will must have two witnesses. The usual answer is the sanction of nullity, but we shall deal later with that sanction and this point (*post*, p. 90).

2.   Repealing laws. These, it is said, are not commands. Even Austin (Lect. 1 *in fin.*) treats these as exceptions. As permission to do a thing is a command to people generally not to interfere with the doing, it seems easy to answer that a repealing statute, by destroying the permissions or prohibitions of the earlier law, has created new prohibitions or permissions and thus is a com-

mand. It is objected (see Brown, *Austinian Theory of Law*, p. 339) that these exist not by virtue of the repealing statute but by virtue of the law existing before the repealed statute was made. Tindall C.J., in Kay *v.* Goodwin (6 Bingham 582), is cited as saying that the effect of repeal is to make the repealed statute as if it had never been, except as to those actions which were begun and completed while it was existing law. This does not seem to negative the view that it was the repealing statute which revived the old law and so commanded, and the other view seems more subtle than sound. The rights and duties did not exist immediately before the repealing statute was passed, and it gave legal force to the old rules. It is a kind of legislation by reference and is the command. The case may not, however, be quite simple. If a restrictive statute is repealed, the old law is restored, but what is the effect on acts done contrary to the statute now repealed, while it was in force? If they can no longer be proceeded against, it may be said that this must be by virtue of the old law, not by virtue of an Act passed after the thing was done. That does not seem to be material. The liberty did not exist till the repealing statute was passed and then did. It seems that it was created by the statute acting retrospectively. In fact most statutes are repealing statutes. If they do not repeal a statute, they commonly repeal in part some prohibition or command of the common law. The same point does not arise there, as there is no earlier rule to be revived by the repeal. Yet it is not obvious why the repeal should be a command in the one case and not in the other. Brown (*loc. cit.*) considers a statute repealing one against gambling and asks if we are to say that in such a case gambling is permissible; 'the theory of English law', he says, 'would be better expressed by saying that there was, but is no longer, a rule of law with regard to gambling'. It seems to me that Brown's very proper objection to gambling leads him to an impossible position. He goes on to say that if, after the repeal, certain persons choose to gamble and others interfere, this interference will be taken notice of not by virtue of the repealing statute but by virtue of the existing law about assaults, etc. But it was the new statute which brought the interference under the old law, and that is command. That because the statute against gambling is repealed there is now no law about gambling, and therefore no implied permission to gamble, is a hard saying. Are we to hold that the law does not permit unless the conduct is somewhere mentioned? Should we not rather say that the law permits any conduct which it does not avoid or in some way penalise? *Non omne quod licet honestum est.* We cannot make the distinction turn on our approval or disapproval of the conduct. If, in absence of a statute, there is no implied permission to gamble, no doubt immoral conduct, the same must be true of the most moral doings. There can be no implied permission to relieve distress or to give a wayfarer a lift. There was once a statute, now repealed, against export of textiles from Ireland to England. Is there now no implied permission to export them? (See May, *Constitutional History of England*, III, pp. 305 *sqq.*) It is said that where a woman was brought before a certain J.P. on a summons for assaulting another woman with a saucepan, his worship dismissed the summons on the ground that, having studied Stone's *Justices' Manual* from end to end, he had found no law about saucepans. Is not this substantially the same position?

3. Declaratory statutes are also treated as exceptions. Those which merely repeat an existing prohibition create no new obligation, but it is not unexampled in private life for orders to be repeated. A consolidating Act usually repeats many prohibitions, but as it also usually repeals the old statutes no question arises. Some statutes make no change in the command, but vary the sanction. This is at least a repetition of the command. Where the old statute was obscure it may fairly be said that, so far as it was not known what the law was under it, the new statute makes new law. It certainly does if the old one, because of its obscurity, has not been acted on or if it puts a new interpretation on the law. If it merely confirms the existing interpretation, it is again repeated command.

4.   These are trivialities; the difficult case is that of custom. (See Allen, *Law in the Making*, chh. i, ii.) Speaking only of local customs, ancient or presumed to be, enforced if they satisfy certain requirements, the question is how these, never expressly commanded, and operating long before any question arose of enforcing them in the King's Courts, can be commands of the Sovereign. The difficulty leads many writers to the view that the custom is not law until it has been enforced by the Courts—till then it was only a 'persuasive' source of law. Austin (*op. cit.* (ed. 4), I, p. 37) tells us that the decision of a judge enforcing such a custom is a sovereign command by delegate, a particular command, but, as it involves that the custom will be enforced in future, in effect a general command. But he adds that until it has been so enforced it is only a rule of morality which may become a source of law. This is unsatisfactory. Suppose a custom has been observed in a particular manor from time immemorial. One day it is disputed, and the Court, for the first time, declares it valid. It is now law. On this analysis it was not law before. Customs usually conflict with common law. If the custom was not law, the common law was. Thus the decision which established the custom as law, by that very act declared all previous operations as unlawful. That is not so. No doubt money paid under the custom might not be recoverable, having been paid under error of law. But we have in that case and on this view to consider the payee as sheltering himself behind a rather shabby defence. We know that he is doing nothing of the kind. (The case would look a little better if Austin had said that the customs became law on the first occasion on which a Court enunciated and applied the rules according to which customs would be enforced. We do not know when that was, but it was so long ago as to deprive the question of any practical importance; but the logic of it would still be no better.) It may be objected that the same point arises in all judicial legislation. No one supposes that it was law before the new decision, but the new doctrine will be applied to cases coming later before the Court,

though the facts occurred before the reforming decision. It is *ex post facto* legislation and the same might be thought true of the decision on a custom. But there is a fundamental difference. The effect of a decision introducing new doctrine is to declare wrong, not in accordance with law, what people have been doing and regarding as law. The effect of a decision confirming a custom is to shew that what people had been doing was in accordance with law. The same analysis can hardly apply to both cases. It is only where the custom is declared invalid that there is any real analogy. In any case it is legal fiction; it is magic, not history. Omnipotence cannot undo the past. The act either was or was not in accord with law when it was done.

Why people follow the custom may be immaterial, but it must be an error to say with Austin (*op. cit.* II, p. 553) that the custom has been obeyed in the past owing to the force of public opinion. Many customs are oppressive. It was not public opinion that made copyholders pay high fines—they were imposed on them by the lords. They obeyed the custom because the law was behind the custom. If an alleged customary fine is declared invalid, it ceases to be paid, not because of any change in public opinion, but because the law is not behind it.

Holland (*op. cit.* p. 51) supplements Austin's analysis. The Courts enforce the custom prospectively and retrospectively, so far implying that it was law before it was enforced. That is legal fiction. It cannot have been both law and not law. Brown remarks that it proves nothing; new precedents are retrospective, but no one holds that they were law before. Holland is silent on customs which have operated peacefully without litigation. Brown holds (*op. cit.* p. 313) that Austin is right; custom is a mere persuasive source of law. The existence of a custom is a state of facts which leads the Court to lay down a certain rule. The judge accepts the custom as the basis of his decision much as in other cases he decides on grounds of convenience or the like. He admits that all this fails if the judge must follow the custom. He holds that he need not, but defers to it, if it satisfies certain requirements, just as, though perhaps in a higher degree than, he defers to opinions of writers and to American decisions. He says, 'The fact that the judges often base their decision on custom is paralleled by the fact that they often base their decisions on convenience. In determining the significance of such action, we must remember that, in the unideal world in which we live, justice is wider than law, that much to which judges pay deference is in no way law, and does not even of necessity become law as a result of the judicial decision.' This last remark may perhaps give a clue to the solution of the problem, though neither Brown nor Markby, who says something of the same kind (*Elements of Law*, pp. 12 *sq.*), works it out any further. It is inconsistent with Brown's attitude to Austin, whom he holds to be sound, and we will deal only with his defence of Austin. To shew that judges are not bound by custom, but only defer to it, he points out that there are differences of opinion as to the tests which a custom must satisfy. This is immaterial; there are many points of law on which there is disagreement. It in no way proves custom to be only a persuasive source of law. For, in so far as there is uncertainty, in so far as the requirements are not known, they can no more be persuasive than they can be binding. Brown seems to hold that the fact that they must satisfy certain requirements shews that they are not law. Municipal bye-laws must be reasonable, but they are law. Brown answers: 'Yes! but customs must be proved to be reasonable: bye-laws bind unless proved to be unreasonable.' This may be true, but it is an immaterial distinction for present purposes. The difference cannot turn on burden of proof. Public general statutes do not need to be proved; private Acts commonly do, but are none the less law. But a more important point remains. In the contention that the judge's deference to custom is of the same kind as his deference to a text-writer, and his action, in face of a custom, similar to his acting on the view of a text-writer, he ignores a most vital difference. Judges often decide on the ground of convenience or a *dictum* or the like, but also they still more often decide in a particular way because there is a statute or a decision which deals with the point. Brown would assuredly not hold that, here too, the judge only voluntarily defers. The question is: To which group does his decision in favour of a custom belong, that in which he is bound or that in which he voluntarily defers? The answer is plain. The judge does not decide on grounds of convenience, etc., if there is a clear rule of common law the other way. But in validating a local custom he always does this; it is the nature of custom to override the common law. A judge does not defer to something contrary to common law unless he must. The inference is that he is bound. It seems to follow that it was already law and we are back to the question how it can be thought of as a command.

It may be that as political societies and their institutions do not arise *uno ictu* but gradually crystallise out of a chaos, and since the Courts have over and over again laid down the requirements, such customs as satisfy them are, it may be said, law nowadays. How and when they came to be so may be a question not unlike that of priority between the chicken and the egg. But is there not another way out? The judges apply rules which are not law; the rules of arithmetic are not law. The terms of a contract are not law. But there is a rule of law that agreements having certain characteristics shall be enforced. May we not then say that the decision of the judge is merely the unearthing of such a custom? On this view, what is law is not the custom but the statement of the characteristics which it must have.

The 'general custom of the realm', which Coke identifies with the common law, is hardly custom at all. Some of it no doubt began as local custom which, by the action of the king's justices, became general. It is idle to ask whether this custom was law before the judges laid hands on it, for no judge would then have said that the king or anybody else could make what law he liked. Modern analysis does not apply to it. Nowadays common law is made by the Courts. A new rule is recognised as new and the common law is forthwith so far altered. The judges are feigned to be applying the law when they are actually making it, and everybody knows that, as to facts occurring before the decision, it is *ex post facto* legislation. But we shall not discuss precedent. (See Allen, *op. cit.* chh. 3, 4.)

The law merchant is a different matter. The Courts apply custom known to be observed by the mercantile community in mercantile transactions without reference to antiquity, much of the custom coming from abroad. It is not the same as trade usages. In any case in which a usage is known to prevail in transactions among members of the trade these usages are implied terms in their contracts with each other, though not mentioned on the face of the contract. This is matter of contract. The law merchant is a different thing. In the Middle Ages when most important business was done at the great fairs, to which came merchants of all lands, a law was needed which should be common to them all. This became, at a time too early for modern analysis, what Holdsworth calls a kind of *ius gentium* (*Hist. of English Law*, i, ch. vii). At first enforced apparently only in the market courts it was gradually adopted by the common law Courts and now constitutes part of the common law, being added to from time to time. No present-day purpose is served by calling it custom.

Of those who reject the Austinian conception of law (the command theory) as inadequate or incorrect some think it essential to state the purpose, as part of the definition of law, with or without the element of compulsion, and others, throwing Austin over altogether, say that the binding force of law is due to its acceptance by the people. Something must be said of both these points of view.

PURPOSE. We may recall the view of Vinogradoff, important as that of a great legal historian (see *ante*, pp. 33, 39), who held that compulsion is no essential of law and that purpose is, but nevertheless, in defining law for our times, includes compulsion and omits purpose. But where he is maintaining that compulsion is no necessary part of the law (*op. cit.* ch. ii) he is not confusing the real and the ideal, but reading history and following Maine, shewing that Austin's analysis has not been always and everywhere applicable, though he does not bring out the point made by Jenks (*Law and Politics in the Middle Ages*, p. 3) that the conception of law itself may change in the course of things.

If we accept the Austinian analysis as correct for our day and place, and also hold, as Austin would certainly have admitted, that law is more than mere command, that, as it is, it results from a long evolution, influenced by local, racial, climatic and economic conditions, we are still unsatisfied. We have defined law; we know how the content of a system of law came to be what it is, but we cannot help asking for something more, for some central notion which shall account not only for the binding force of law, but also for its content. It may be doubted whether the quest can be successful. The legal philosopher finds it indeed in purpose, but he is usually dealing with ideal systems which give him a free hand to choose what purpose he will. His results have little relation to actual law. It is true that Ihering, not only a legal philosopher, but a great lawyer also, in his *Zweck im Recht*, lays it down that to understand law, its growth and its future, you must study its purpose, but he is far from holding that all law has one purpose. And the plain lawyer cannot get away from the fact that the characteristic of all municipal law, deeper than commandedness, may not be, and in fact is not, a purpose. Neither the immediate nor the remoter objects of all legislators have been the same. Nor can we say that, however aberrant a particular rule may be, we must take the thing as a whole and consider the general purpose of a system of law. Not all systems of law have had the same social purpose in view, and the same society has had different purposes at different times. Moreover the analytical lawyer must take these aberrant rules into consideration, for, after all, they are law. It may be said that this objection is not tenable. Nature every now and then produces a five-legged calf. None the less the zoologist does not hesitate to describe the calf as a four-legged animal. That is the normal case. May we not say the same of laws? But the cases are not parallel. The fifth leg of the calf is not functional; the aberrant law is. If nature produced occasionally calves with five genuine working legs, the definition would have to be modified. The five-legged calf is recognised at once by all as the monstrosity it is. But different legislatures and the same legislature at different times have had different aims. Philosophers are not agreed as to the proper aims of legislation. The result is that almost any law may be a monstrosity from the point of view of one politician or philosopher and normal from that of another. Till there is agreement as to this purpose (which is not to be expected in the immediate future) the lawyer, bound by the law as it is, must ignore these conflicting views from Nazism and Communism on the one hand to Auberon Herbert's 'Voluntary State' on the other. He has to consider what rules the Court will enforce, for these are the law. No doubt he must consider the purpose of any statute or rule with which he is at the moment dealing, but to-morrow he will be dealing with another statute or rule and the purpose of that may be entirely different.

We can reach a rather pedestrian conception of law, stopping short of ultimate purposes. We may say that the law is the instrument by which the community is held together as a political society. Law has always been the cement of society; so soon as it falls into disregard, civilisation is in danger. But that too is insufficient. It tells us what the law has done, but no more. Order is the means, not the end. But if we seek to go further, as lawyers, we are compelled to say that the characteristic we are seeking will vary in different cases according to the prepossessions of the legislator when the particular piece of legislation was enacted, i.e. in democracies, the state of public opinion at the time.

Kant, dealing with an ideal, introduced a theory which may be regarded as expressing a purpose, the *Willenstheorie*, which has much influenced modern thought. The rule of law gives effect to each man's will so far as this is consistent with equal freedom of other men's wills, according to a universal law of freedom (*Philosophy of Right*, Hastie's translation, p. 45). But he is clear that he is not dealing with actual law; he says that the actual content of any system may not agree in the least with this (*op. cit.* p. 44). Hegel modifies this, but his world process, evolving liberty, making a sort of fusion of the ideal and the actual, seems to add but little to Kant, for present purposes, beyond a note of optimism. Nineteenth-century pandectists went further, and wove this notion into their expositions of the actual law. From Regelsberger (*Pandekten*) it is difficult to get more than Gilbert's 'law is the pure embodiment of everything that is excellent'. For Dernburg (*Pandekten*, 1, § 19) the law is the *allgemeine Wille*, which is not true. Even in a democracy it can only be the will of the majority of the moment, and it is not true at all in a despotism established by force. Windscheid (*Pandektenrecht*) is more systematic. In his *allgemeiner Teil* the whole actual law is deduced from the *Willenstheorie*. It is dexterously done and very unconvincing; the rules might equally well have been deduced from another philosophy. It in no way expresses the Roman Law to which he seeks to apply it.

The attempt to base actual law on a purpose is essentially a failure to distinguish, even to see that there is a distinction, between positive law and that conceivable law reached by philosophical enquiry. The fallacy is crystallised by including in the definition of law qualities which the framers think desirable (they are apt to say essential) qualities of law. It is easy to define law as, say, a rule laid down by society, aiming at self-development of citizens, or at giving the fullest possible expression to their wills, or at producing from each the greatest possible contribution to the well-being of the society, or at justice, or at the greatest happiness of the greatest number, or what you will.[1]

1 All these are 'good', and they are not independent; they interlock. Each of them to some extent forwards each of the others. But these 'ideologies' are in books. They remain ideals. Those which have been formally adopted in practice by certain nations are of a very different

None of these is true of the whole content of any system of laws that ever existed. Some rules would pass all these tests; others would pass none. Many laws have been kept in force because they benefited powerful classes, e.g. copyhold. Sooner or later, of course, such things go in most communities, but *non constat* that they are not replaced by others. While they exist the proposed definitions of law are false, regarded as definitions of the law of the land. What is and what ought to be are not the same, even though the philosophers were agreed as to the social purpose, which they are not. Even that the law is approximating to the ideal is not necessarily true, especially in autocracies, unless we believe all dictators to be well-informed, high-minded philanthropists, which does not seem to be true. There is indeed Green's way out of the difficulty, the heroic way of denying the facts. Having a definition of the State which included moral ends, he found it impossible to bring Czarist Russia within its terms. Accordingly he said that Czarist Russia was not a State at all (*ante*, p. 34). That is to deny plain facts. Czarist Russia was a State, and however much we may detest the doings of some more recent dictators, the communities which they controlled were in fact States. Similarly, to say that a law is not a law unless it aims at what one thinks right is confused thinking, with the effect of a falsehood. Since philosophers are by no means agreed, it would follow that if there was anything in the community which they would call law at all there would be as many systems of law in the community as there were schools of political philosophy. *Quod est absurdum.*

ACCEPTANCE. If purpose will not serve us as the rational basis of actual law, what are we to say of acceptance (to which

character. The Nazi ideal was to fit the German people for world domination by conquest. The Italian, more moderate, was military achievement and the aggrandisement of the Italian Empire. These appear to be quite irreconcilable. No doubt Hitler and Mussolini might claim to have one or other of the further ideals behind them: conquest being only a means to that end. They produced nothing but misery.

Dernburg's 'General Will', just mentioned, is an approximation) as the test, the doctrine that law owes its validity to the
fact that it is accepted by those who are to be bound by it?
We are told that a law does not become law by enactment, but
by acceptance, or as Vinogradoff puts it (*Common Sense in Law*,
p. 39) by recognition. This is a variant of the Social Contract
theory to which we shall recur, a contract renewed on every
new piece of legislation. It is difficult to see much force in this.
There is of course a sense in which it is true; a man does not
become Sovereign by saying that he is. If people do not habitually
obey his commands he is not Sovereign and his commands are
not laws. But in the only sense in which it is relevant to our
discussion, i.e. in the sense that observance by the people implies
acceptance and so makes it law, it is not in the least true. Some
years ago the present writer heard this doctrine very clearly
expounded and applied to the speed-limit rule, which, it was
said, was not law, because it was not accepted by those whom it
was meant to bind. A few days later *The Times* contained an
analysis of motoring offences in a certain area. Of these one-
fifth were for exceeding the speed limit. It does not seem that
any of the motorists pleaded that there was no such law or would
have succeeded if they had, but if the speaker did not mean that
they were unjustly deprived of their money it is difficult to see
what he did mean. The rule was certainly not very well enforced
because there was no powerful element in the community which
was interested in its enforcement. The Volstead Act in America
was not well enforced because there was a powerful element in
the community which was interested in its non-enforcement.
There are, it is said, areas in which murder commonly goes
unpunished: that does not alter the fact that there is a law against
murder there. Even if a law is totally unobserved, that does
not shew that it is not law. In some communities this is provided
for; a certain period of non-observance nullifies the statute. This
is not so with us. However dead and gone a rule may appear
to be, Ashford *v.* Thornton (1 Bar. and Ald. p. 405) warns us

against saying that it is not law. The proposition would not even look true anywhere but in a democracy. The laws of Czarist Russia were not accepted by the people: they were enforced on the people by means of the organised force which is so much more effective than the unorganised force of the masses. They were commands of a superior in exactly Austin's sense. But it is not true even for a democracy. There are always laws which the Courts disapprove and enforce reluctantly. There are always unpopular rules which the people do not want but which are enforced. This view, however, differs fundamentally from Duguit's. For the view now under consideration, any rule actually enforced is law, apparently because that implies acceptance, which it does not in the least. For Duguit this fact is irrelevant; it is not law unless it subserves the social purpose, whatever that may be.

Vinogradoff, dealing with acceptance, commits himself to some questionable propositions. He says (*op. cit.* p. 39) that law 'depends ultimately on recognition. Such recognition is a legal act, although the enforcement of a recognised rule may depend on moral restraint, the fear of public opinion, or, eventually, the fear of a popular rising.' Unless this means that recognition was an agreed act, but its consequences are only compelled by force, which is not true historically, it makes the consent a mere fiction. Recognition is not distinguishable from obedience. He gives illustrations to shew that the law does not depend on coercive sanctions. The German Kaiser, he says (p. 38), was under the Constitution enjoined not to do certain things, but could not be compelled. So far as concerns the things he could not do there is no great difficulty; he could not declare war without a vote of the Reichstag, but that means only that the declaration of war would not be a State act. If the army followed him, this would be revolution. And since proceedings would presumably lie against persons who carried out unauthorised orders of the Kaiser, they were commands to the general public though not to the Kaiser. As to positive acts, if the Constitution provided machinery for his removal, for omissions, these rules would be sanctioned, but as it did not, and no other remedy seems to have existed, he was simply above the law and no real purpose is served by calling such pious opinions laws, even though they were enshrined in the Constitution. Again, he says (p. 41), suppose a civil wrong against me by one who has no money. There is no real sanction. Is there no law? There is no force in this. There is of course the sanction of bankruptcy and other inconveniences, but the important point is that the fact that circumstances enable an individual, on occasion, to evade the sanction, does not alter the fact that there is one. A dying man can murder with impunity. It is the more odd that he should have taken this line, as, elsewhere (p. 52), he clearly brings out this point. His conclusions are in fact inconsistent. Just as he follows his proposition that compulsion is not essential to law with a definition which includes it, so here, not only is there the inconsistency just noted, but when he comes to speak of international law (p. 41) he calls it imperfect law, precisely, it seems, because it is without means of enforcement.

We have already spoken of the old notion that all legal rights and duties are based on a convention, the Social Contract. Everyone knows that in historical fact there was no such thing. We must remember that our law, with others, at one time found difficulty in founding legal obligation on anything but convention. What is best called quasi-contract our lawyers call contract implied in law, though there is no agreement. It is possible to see something of this kind in legal history. If one settles in an area occupied by other people, one may be said to be bound by quasi-contract to observe their customs. That wide sense may have something to do with the persistence and ready acceptance of the Social Contract. There are, however, distinguished writers who, admitting that there never was a Social Contract, yet find it a necessary factor in their explanation of society. Professor Barker says (*op. cit.* p. 166): 'Maine does not disprove the doctrine of natural right and the social contract by alleging that "history shews" society beginning not with individual rights but with group-status, and not with free contract but with paternal power...in any case the apostles of natural right and social contract were not concerned with historical origins. They were thinking not of the chronological antecedents but of the logical presuppositions of a political society. They meant that they could only explain society if they presupposed contracting individuals with individual rights, just as most of us would say that we can only explain the whole world of human life if we presuppose a God. The latter presupposition would not be invalidated, if historians amassed a thousand instances of primitive tribes who knew no god. The former presupposition is not invalidated by a thousand instances of primitive paternal power. It can only be invalidated by proof either that it fails to explain what it has to explain, or that this can be explained otherwise, and such a proof, though it is possible, is not possible to history.'

Whatever Professor Barker says calls for attention and respect, but it is submitted that this is not a satisfactory account of the matter. Maine did not merely 'allege' the patriarchal theory— he set out to prove it. Whether he did or not is another matter. A necessary logical presupposition which is not true cannot be an explanation of anything. The explanation of the monthly new moon offered by certain African philosophers is, we are told, that the sun eats the old one, whereupon the responsible authority makes another. This is commonly rejected in Europe because it is not true and it would probably still be rejected even though our astronomers offered no other. An explanation which is not true is not mended by the absence of a better. If a contract which never was is a necessary logical presupposition for a certain theory of the State, that theory is incorrect and the allegation of a contract is no explanation. The analogy with savage communities who knew no god is quite unconvincing. That they did not know there was a god did not of course prove that there was none. But Maine did not say that early communities did not know there was a contract; he said, rightly or wrongly, that there was none. If the savages had possessed proof that there was no god, the theological view of the universe would have been destroyed. Professor Barker's view is a modern rationalisation. On the evidence it seems that early writers on the Social Contract really did believe there was a contract, blinding themselves to its impossibility. This 'explanation' is not science; it is analogous to what is called popular science. What these writers say, in effect, is: 'In order that you may understand the working of the social system, let us suppose that at the beginning all the people met and agreed on the rules which should govern their relations. Of course they did not, but supposing they had done so and society went on, you would get just the state of things which now exists. Society works as if there had been a social contract.' An imaginary state of things is suggested to facilitate the understanding of what exists. This is what is done in manuals of popular science. The real explanation being too hard for the lay reader, an analogy is put to him by which he can get some idea of the phenomenon. Thus in a little book on Economics (*Cash and Credit*, pp. 22 *sqq.*) the author, Mr D. A. Barker, is seeking to shew how a credit system increases the effectiveness of the money really available. He illustrates credit by supposing a cylinder with water, representing money, in it, and, under the surface of this, a concealed rubber bag. The bag represents credit. The more you blow it out the more money there seems to be.[1] For the purpose it is an apt illustration, but it is not a scientific explanation, and it would never have occurred to the author to call it the 'Theory of the Expanding Bag' (even though we have seen the dodge of the legal fiction erected into the 'Philosophy of the *als ob*'). The author has the real explanation in mind, but thinks the readers for whom the book is designed would not understand it, or will understand it better with the help of the parable. But our social philosophers have no further explanation; it is, they say, the only way in which they can understand society. Mathematicians use irrational quantities in their calculations, but

1 See Addison, *Spectator*, No. 3.

they eliminate them; they do not leave an irrational quantity in their final result. In fact, political science postulates a political society. It is for history to say how it came into existence, though Professor Barker says it cannot do so. But to account for the existence of States and their law is not to justify them, and the latter is the aim of these philosophies. The Social Contract is another attempt to find a rational basis for law, worse than most of them, as it is certainly untrue.

VI

Particular and General Jurisprudence

Is there such a thing as 'Particular Jurisprudence', the Jurisprudence of a particular system? We speak of abstract or pure Jurisprudence which deals with the fundamental principles of all systems of law, and is sometimes called 'General Jurisprudence'. No man knows all systems, and, for us, this means western systems and their derivatives, sometimes called mature systems. There could hardly be a more unsuitable word, for there are eastern systems which were old when we were barbarians. In fact, short of abstract Jurisprudence, there may be as many jurisprudences as there are groupings of States. In practice there would be only two in the west—those based on Roman Law and those based on Germanic Law, though some, like modern German Law, are hybrids. Austin contrasts this with Particular Jurisprudence, the underlying notions of any one system of law. It is objected that this is only the study of law, of a system of law, from a particular point of view. That is true, but it is no objection. It is an attempt to arrive at the underlying principles and broadest generalisations of the system. The *allgemeiner Teil* of a treatise on *Pandektenrecht* is essentially Particular Jurisprudence, though, as we have seen, writers seek to give it a 'general' air by introducing into it the *Willenstheorie*. The finest piece of work ever done in this kind was Ihering's *Geist des römischen Rechts*. General Jurisprudence is an attempt to do the same thing in a wider field; it is an attempt to expound the fundamental principles and broadest generalisations of two or more systems, the study of those systems from a particular point of view. But these generalisations will not be the same as those of Particular Jurisprudence.

Professor Holland made objections, holding that such a study could not be a science (*op. cit.* pp. 9 *sqq.*). Considerably more than half a century ago the present writer made a brief reply to these objections (*Law Quart. Rev.* 1890, p. 445). He sees nothing to alter in what he then said. Holland compares geology. The geology of England is not distinct from general geology: it is a part of that science. He says, 'A science is a system of generalisations which, though they may be derived from observations over a limited area, will hold good everywhere, assuming the object-matter of the science to possess everywhere the same characteristics'; and, again, 'Principles of Geology elaborated from the observation of England alone hold good all over the globe, in so far as the same substances and forces are everywhere present, and the principles of Jurisprudence, if arrived at entirely from English data, would be true if applied to the particular laws of any other community of human beings, assuming them to resemble in essentials the human beings who inhabit England.' These are remarkable propositions. Whether we call it a science or not is immaterial: the question is whether it is Jurisprudence and distinct from General Jurisprudence. Holland refuses the name Jurisprudence to it on the ground of the impropriety of describing such empirical knowledge by a term which should be used only as descriptive of a science. Why Particular Jurisprudence should be empirical and practical in a derogatory sense is not clear: these are odd epithets to apply, for instance, to such work as Ihering's *Geist*. A study involving extraction of generalisations from an observed mass of facts has a scientific method. When the facts are laws and the generalisations are fundamental propositions it is Jurisprudence. It may be that Holland is a little influenced by the notion of an ideal law, which might be thought to be universal, like Kant's, though even that universality may be doubtful. His provisos are important: 'assuming the object-matter of the science to possess everywhere the same characteristics', 'in so far as the same substances and forces are everywhere present', 'assuming them to resemble in essentials the human beings who inhabit England'. But what if the object-matter of the science does not possess everywhere the same characteristics? How if the same forces are not present? How if the other community does not resemble England in essentials? And what are essentials? Nothing is more certain than that the fundamental notions of law have not been the same in all times and places, as indeed Holland admits in the remarks which follow these propositions. The propositions seem nevertheless to rest on the notion of a necessary law which is the same everywhere. Such a notion is inconsistent with the true conception of law as being in a great degree the product of the milieu in which it has developed. The analogy with geology is as misleading as analogies commonly are. If the geology of England is not a distinct science, this is because it contains nothing which is not contained in general geology, though its record is less complete. This is not true of law. Some principles of French Law run counter to the English Law. Such divergent principles cannot be a part of General Jurisprudence, but they are of Particular Jurisprudence. Law is not a mechanical structure, like geological deposits: it is a growth and its true analogy is with biology. The general laws are laws of development and suggest, not abstract Jurisprudence, but historical and comparative Jurisprudence. Holland meets this by saying that both sciences are progressive. This is true, but they are progressive in different senses. In Jurisprudence, principles which were once true are not true now. In geology, principles which were once thought to be true are now known not to be true. That is a very different thing. Dr Allen (*Legal Duties*, p. 9) defends Holland's view that Jurisprudence is progressive and treats the present writer as denying this. But what it was sought to shew was that it is progressive in another sense. No doubt it is in fact progressive in both senses.

The basis of General Jurisprudence is that there are general principles common to western systems. That cannot rank as an axiom. Where is the necessary proof? If we say it rests on the law of nature, we need go no further, but we have seen where that leads (*ante*, p. 34). Austin takes it on faith, for he speaks of 'necessary notions, principles and distinctions' (*op. cit.* II, p. 1108), which language is so like that associated with the law of nature that some foreign writers treat Austin as a disguised supporter of the doctrine of *Naturrecht*. But it can be shewn by investigation that there are principles found in all these systems. Their bulk is not great. As they all admit the notion of compulsion, of the law as command or the like, they all have command, duty, and sanction. Duty implies rights, not necessarily private rights (see *post*, pp. 92 *sqq.*), since all duties might be due to and enforceable by the State alone. Duty implies neglect of duty, voluntary action, and the distinction between wilfulness and negligence. These notions and some others do in fact exist everywhere. The distinction, if it is one, between State rights and private rights is found everywhere. So is that between civil and criminal remedies. The distinction between rights *in rem* and rights *in personam*, in some form, exists everywhere, though it is challenged by some moderns, and a system might exist without it. But this does not amount to much, and a book dealing with these alone and only so far as they were material to the study of the law would not be very big. There are other general notions of a different stamp, such as consent, intent, will and so forth. These of course admit of long discussion. They cover for instance the field of theoretical psychology. Much of Austin's lectures on 'pervading notions' consists of slight, inconclusive discussions of that topic, of which Pollock says somewhere that it is 'cumbrous rubbish'. It may be noted that very few of the ideas which Austin calls 'necessary' or universal are peculiar to Jurisprudence. They form part of the common stock of ideas, but have not much closer connection with law than have the rules of arithmetic, which the Courts have, from time to time, occasion to apply. Other sciences have many principles of which it may be said that no one apart from students of that science has any knowledge, or conception, of their meaning. In General Jurisprudence the notions of that kind are for the most part little more than matters of classification. The case is different with

Particular Jurisprudence. Anyone who has made the attempt will know how difficult it is to explain to an English lawyer the ideas behind a Roman technical term, or to make a foreigner from a civil law country understand our peculiar conceptions. Law contains a number of general propositions. Those found in independent systems may be called General Jurisprudence. Those peculiar to one system are Particular Jurisprudence. Holland's view that there are no principles peculiar to one system of law (and no other contention will serve his purpose) is an error. It may almost be said that Particular Jurisprudence is the more important and General Jurisprudence (as opposed to philosophy of law) something of a pretender. Most English writers deal with Particular Jurisprudence. Austin in fact does, for though he claims universality for his conclusions, he finds them almost entirely in English Law. Pollock and Salmond are expressly devoted to the common law; other systems appear only by way of illustration. Even Holland, purporting uncompromisingly to be general, deals mainly with common law. Hearn is almost entirely common law. Lightwood has a wider range, but his subject is not abstract Jurisprudence but historical and comparative, a much more fruitful field. Of more recent works, Professor Allen's *Law in the Making*, a work on sources of law, is not a general treatise on Jurisprudence, still less a treatise on General Jurisprudence. It is comparative and takes a wide sweep, though, in an English book, intended mainly for English readers, English Law has naturally the greatest prominence. Professor Keeton's *Elements of Jurisprudence* purports indeed to be 'general' —we are told in the preface that the fundamental principles of law are constant—but the actual treatment is highly comparative, the author having effectively used his own experience, gained under different systems in the East and in the West.

Holland describes Jurisprudence as the 'formal science of positive law'. For the non-philosophical reader this is rather cryptic. It may be taken to mean that Jurisprudence is concerned only with the fundamental conceptions of law and not with its actual content, the detailed rules which are based on these conceptions, or (it is the same thing in other words) the detailed rules from which these principles can be deduced. It seems not impossible that Holland, in rejecting Particular Jurisprudence, is really thinking not so much of Jurisprudence itself as of the prolegomena of Jurisprudence, the question what we mean when we say 'a law'. It may be that the answer to this question is, in western communities, everywhere the same. So far there could be no 'particular' science, but this has no relation to the question whether the fundamental notions of systems of law are everywhere the same. It is submitted that they are not.

VII

The State

AUSTIN'S 'Sovereign' is the legislator. He deals with the body which makes the law and with nothing else. He does not usually talk about the State. Many who profess to adopt or to state Austin's view make the law a rule enforced by the State. This substitution has had a bad effect on the argument because of the elusive nature of the notion 'State'. The substitution is caused by the difficulty found in applying the notion 'command', and the fact that there are communities in which there is no Austinian Sovereign. But it avoids the difficulty only by introducing a certain vagueness. For, what is the State? It is not quite easy to see what T. H. Green (*op. cit.* §§ 80–136) means by the State. Some of his language seems to suggest that the State is the whole body for whose well-being the organised society exists, i.e. the community. But on the whole he seems to mean the entire governmental apparatus, of which, he says, the law-maker, the Sovereign, is an institution (§ 132). He is of course talking politics, not law. Thus he places the power of command not in the Sovereign behind whom the lawyer cannot go, but in the 'general will', in 'that impalpable congeries of the hopes and fears of a people, bound together by common interests and sympathy, which we call the general will' (§ 86). This too is a rather elusive conception. It is not the will of all, we are told, nor even necessarily the will of a majority. This seems to mean that in a typical State the governmental system is able to endure because it is approved by the mass of the people, or, if they do not positively approve it, yet, by reason of their love of country and desire for maintenance of their national life, they are prepared to put up with it. This may be true, but, if said of all States, it is a fiction. If a people does not like the system of government and still does not destroy it, this will often be because the organised force at the command of the Government is stronger than the unorganised strength of the people, and the more efficient a Government is the less ground there is for saying that it rests on the general will. The Russian people several times revolted unsuccessfully against its Government. Finally, when the Government had its hands full it was destroyed by revolution. The general will could, at long last, destroy, but it could not reconstruct. The present Government no more rests on the general will than did that of the Czar. Sidgwick (*Elements of Politics*) seems to see in the State, as holder of the public rights, something narrower than the State considered as the whole community (p. 211), but does not say what this narrower State is. But his view does not concern us. He does not regard legislative power as in the State; with Austin he puts legal sovereignty in the legislature. Hearn, defining law as command of the State, expressly refuses to define this State (*op. cit.* p. 5), but adds that it expresses what in popular language is called the Government. This is explaining *obscurum per obscurius*, for this word may mean the ministry, or the executive, or the whole governmental machinery. He probably means the last, but none of the three is Sovereign in the sense of the legislator, and the one thing that people never mean by Government is the Parliament, which in fact does make law. It is impossible to tell from Spencer's *The Man* versus *the State* whether for him the State is the Government, the Parliament, the electorate or something else. Brown (*op. cit.* pp. 270 *sqq.*), talking political science rather than law, seems to accept Green's analysis and find supremacy in the general will, and this he locates in 'the State'. But he does not tell us what that is (pp. 279 *sqq.*). It is clearly wider than the electorate (p. 279). He cites (p. 286) Grotius in support of the proposition that the State is the Sovereign, and no doubt Grotius does say that the *civitas* is Sovereign, and describes the *civitas* as the *populus*, which seems to mean everybody (Grotius, *De iure belli ac pacis*, Whewell's transl. I, pp. 113 *sqq.*). But he is really no authority for Brown. He does not indeed free himself from the notion of agreement; no publicist of that age could. But he tells us that it is a blunder to say that in all States the *summa potestas* is in the hands of the people, so that it has the power of controlling kings and punishing them if they abuse their power. For, he says, it is not difficult to conceive causes why a people may resign the whole power of its own Government and transfer it to another, either a body of nobles or a single ruler. And no State was ever so *popularis* that some were not excluded from voting. All this shews how far Grotius was from the doctrine he is cited as supporting. He is discussing the proposition that a war, to be a public war, must be made by the holder of the *summa potestas*, that body whose acts are not subject to another. For him, legislative and executive power are thought of as in the same hands, but, subject to this, his reference to voting shews that the State for Grotius is either the legislature (the Austinian Sovereign) or possibly the electorate which may be called the political Sovereign. But for Brown, and for Green, the State seems to be everybody. Here there is difficulty for Brown, who purports to be analysing existing institutions, though perhaps not for Green, who is really, at bottom, considering the ideal State. If this State, this people wider than the electorate, desires to make a change, how can it act? It is voiceless. Brown sees the difficulty and suggests (p. 283) that as revolution is their only way, the State may have wished itself to proceed only by this way of revolution. But this is mere fiction. A successful revolution is not a political act; it is the destruction of a polity and the creation of another. No State ever so organised itself. The Constitution was to be perpetual, though usually with machinery for amendment in detail. In fact, members of the society, outside the electorate, have no more power in the State than a foreign community has. They may be able to upset the State, though it is not true to say that they usually can, but that is not political power. Foreign powers have often done this, but the foreign power is not the Sovereign of the State. In fact, just as law implies a legal organisation, so politics implies a polity with an organisation. What is outside the organisation has nothing to do with politics, as a descriptive science, though it has to do with political philosophy. If a polity finds itself in need of mending, it may, for instance, enlarge its electorate and introduce new elements into the polity. It will do this for reasons: good administrators will always have the betterment of the polity in view. But it is a confusion between analysis and political ethics which leads to this sort of conception of the State. The same book may discuss both; Sidgwick does, but he never misses the distinction between analysis of existing institutions and the ideal community. An orderly community controlled by a despot with command of extraordinary natural forces would be for him a State, however evil and selfish the despot, but not for Green.

Jenks, in articles in the *Harvard Law Review* (1916–17), discusses the conception of the State, but is more concerned with the danger of treating this entity as the source of law than with defining it. But he is clear that it is not the community. 'The distinction between the community and the artificial entity known as the State must be borne in mind' (p. 121). Apparently he means by it the whole governmental system.

Gray (*Nature and Sources of the Law*) does define the State. He says (ed. 2, p. 65) that it is the artificial person created so that, by assuming it as the entity whose organs are the men engaged in protecting a mass of human beings against fraud and violence, a unity of operation may be given to those organs. This is not very helpful. In terms his definition would cover a trade protection society or a society for the prosecution of felons. But that could be easily amended. The important point is that the definition does not tell us what the State consists of. The State, like a corporation, is an abstraction having no real existence in the physical world. We know or can discover who make up a corporation, but who make up this State? Even if we agree with those who give a corporation a real personality, distinct from those of its members, the fact remains that all acts are done by men. For our purpose it is the organs (if an abstraction can have organs) who are important. Some member or members of that body actually commands and makes law: to say, with such a conception of the State, that the State makes the law, is simply to evade the difficulty of determining who actually does make it.

It is no doubt the elusive nature of the conceptions involved which leads to such differences of opinion, among those who associate law and State, as to the relation between the two notions. For Salmond (*op. cit.* § 36, *init.*) 'it is in and through the State alone that Law exists'. For Mr Hannis Taylor also (*Science of Jurisprudence*, p. 505) 'not until after the State is formed can there be law in the proper sense of the term'. And, though he does not use the word 'State', Hobbes is in the same boat: 'none can make laws but the commonwealth' and 'as the commonwealth is no person and cannot act, it is done by the Sovereign'.[1] But for Professor Laski (*Introd., cit.* p. xvii) 'the rule of law is, clearly, independent of the State and is indeed anterior to it'. According to the institutional theory, says Mr Jennings (*Modern Theories of Law*, p. 81), 'it is not the State which creates the law nor the law which creates the State: they arise simultaneously by the act of foundation'. And this last sentence may serve us as a bridge to the opinion of Kelsen, already considered (*ante*, p. 19), that law and State are the same thing, a view which seems to be shared by Krabbe, in some passages, though elsewhere he holds that law creates the State. For the Jurisprudence of the lawyer these difficulties are unimportant. He observes that laws are made by men or groups of men, and if he finds communities in which certain things cannot be done and laws purporting to do them are void, this too he finds to be due to the dead hand, to a Koran, a Torah, or the Constitution of the U.S.A., all produced under historical conditions which cannot be reproduced, and not to the power of any abstraction. Whether the men who make the laws, and behind

1 *Leviathan*, ch. xxvi (pp. 189, 190, Waller's ed.).

whom he cannot go, are organs or agents of any abstract State or electorate or population is a matter which does not concern him. It is no doubt the influence of Aristotle which makes modern writers on political science include in their definition of a State the end for which in their view the State exists. This forces some of them, as we saw, to deny the name 'State' to a society not organised for that end. But the purpose of the State is no part of its definition for legal purposes. This does not mean that the lawyer has nothing to do with ends. To interpret a statute it is often necessary to know its purpose, and some institutions can hardly be understood apart from the purpose they serve, e.g. the electoral machinery. But the purpose of any statute may well not conform to any preconceived purpose of the State, and it is the former with which he is directly concerned. Every reasonable man will have in mind some at least of the purposes which the State ought to serve, but these form no part of his analysis of the law.

It is a favourite doctrine of one school of writers, hotly contradicted by another, that the State is an organism, all sorts of conclusions being drawn from this. As a preliminary we must know what is a State and what is an organism. We have seen how difficult it is to attach a clear meaning to the word 'State', but we may here assume that it means the political organisation. A student of Jurisprudence cannot be expected to know, of his own knowledge, what is an organism, and scientists, whose business it would seem to be, do not give a very clear answer to the question. Capacity of growth is not enough—crystals grow, but are not organisms. A State shares the power of functioning with no outside aid, but what it can pick up for itself, with clocks constructed to wind themselves up by solar heat. Independent volition cannot be attributed to the lowest biological organisms. But if all this be accepted and an organism be regarded as what combines these characteristics, there is the difficulty that the State differs from organisms in that its parts or organs have independent wills. A man's arm has no will other than the man's, but every man, and perhaps every group, has an independent will of his own. In fact an organism being not capable of exact definition and being a biological notion, the idea is only an analogy, from which it is not permissible to draw conclusions. On the other hand, the conception of the State as a mere mechanism is also an analogy and a less useful one, involving serious error. As Professor Barker says (*op. cit.* p. 107), 'the State is not an organism but it is like an organism'. It has some of the qualities of an organism and the conception is helpful to the understanding of it, of its various activities, of its continuity in change, of the proposition that it is an entity and not a mere collective term, of the doctrine, not universally accepted, that it has a real, not merely a fictitious, personality, and of what are sometimes called the consequences flowing from these propositions, but are better called evidences of this similarity. But the idea should be used for exposition only, and not to prove anything.

VIII

Politics and Polities

IT seems plain that a science of politics should involve polities, but even Sidgwick, though alive to this fact, sometimes uses language which obscures it. He hesitates about the case in which those who call themselves the Government are not obeyed. He observes (*op. cit.* p. 30) that on such facts 'we do not come into serious conflict with common sense by affirming that they do not really govern and that their commands are not laws'. Clearly we should be in conflict with common sense if we said anything else. But, later on (p. 598), he holds that in cases like the Camorra or the Land League, 'if the directions backed by this illegal force were obeyed to anything like the same extent as the directions of Government, we should recognise that the powers belonging to Government had been partially transferred to the illegal directors in a disorderly way'. But, if the orders are illegal, the directors who enforce them are not political authorities. If there is an authority habitually obeyed, it is the political authority, and sporadic revolutionary risings do not affect the matter. But if there is no authority habitually obeyed, but several are 'fighting for the Crown', there is no real political authority. The powers exercised by the illegal directors are not the same as, or part of, those normally exercised by government. In fact he adds on the same page the remark that it may be held that the power thus transferred would not be properly political, on the ground that the 'political' character of a society is lost or impaired when it falls into disorder and anarchy. This seems sounder, except that the word 'impaired' is not adequate. In anarchy there is no polity, no political power. Only when the irregular power has become stable and issues and enforces orders against which the old government is substantially powerless can we speak of it as political. A government may be real though it came into existence by revolution, but till some stability and dominance is reached there is no polity.

Sidgwick's remarks on another group of phenomena seem rather doubtful. Speaking of a king controlled by a priest or a mistress he says (pp. 599 *sqq.*) that their power is political in effect if not in nature. But he holds that if a king abstains from certain acts of legislation for fear of losing his mistress or from fear of extra-mundane penalties threatened by a priest, this is a case in which the will of these persons produces political effects, but we should not affirm a transfer of sovereignty. If, however, a monarch habitually obeys a priest not from fear of these extra-mundane penalties but because the influence of the priest over the people is such that they would certainly obey him rather than the king, we shall agree, says Sidgwick, that he no longer possesses supreme political sovereignty; 'it would hardly be denied that the priest had become really if not nominally the political superior of the monarch'. Is it possible so to distinguish between these cases? Is it possible to say that if the priest threatens the king with Hell the king is still Sovereign, but if he threatens the king with revolution then the priest is the political Sovereign? Governments are over and over again deterred from action by fear of revolution and it does not seem to matter whether it is created by the threat of an individual or is, so to speak, in the air. If under the forms of the Constitution the Courts are bound to obey the king's commands and habitually do so, then he is none the less Sovereign for legal purposes because in given circumstances he is afraid to issue a certain command for fear that the polity, and with it his power, will be destroyed. And if, under the Constitution, he is autocratic, he is the political Sovereign too. The power of Rasputin and his like is extra-political. No one doubts that the Czar was for all purposes, within the polity, Sovereign until the whole society fell to pieces. Of course a revolution is not always blood and fire, and sometimes it is slow. It was a revolution in this country when acts of the king began to require the endorsement of a minister, and, in our hypothetical case, if the Courts took to disregarding ukases till they were countersigned by the priest, we might say that a theocracy had arrived. But not till then.

IX

Legal Sovereign and Political Sovereign

IT is important to distinguish between the legal Sovereign, the authority whose command binds the Courts, i.e. with us, the king in Parliament, and the political Sovereign, the body with which political power finally rests, i.e. with us, the electorate. But Austin oscillates between them, and his language is extraordinarily confusing. He says what may be paraphrased as follows. Where the real Sovereign exercises its powers through representatives it may delegate its powers either subject to a trust or absolutely, in which latter case the elected body is for the time invested completely with sovereign character. This last is the method in which, in this country, the commons delegate their power to the House of Commons. The delegation is absolute. If there were a trust, it might be enforceable by legal or merely by moral sanctions. And this is the position occupied by the House of Commons. They are trustees for the electorate. The notion that the delegation is absolute probably arose from the facts that the trust is tacit and is enforced only by moral sanctions (*op. cit.* pp. 251 *sqq.*).

Thus there is no trust at all, but yet there turns out to be a trust, after all, but one of which the sanction is moral. The beginning and the end are in flat contradiction. The fact is that Austin's mind is not clear on the point. Instead of keeping to the only sense of the word 'Sovereign' which is germane to his topic, the legal Sovereign, he is troubled by the fact that sovereignty can in some sense be attributed to the electorate. In his attempt to reconcile this with a single meaning for the word he throws his whole discussion into confusion. In *Modern Theories of Law*, p. 206, Professor Manning denies the contradiction, but it is there. Austin may have meant what Manning says he did, but it is not what he says. It is true that, as Manning says, Austin does not talk about the legal Sovereign—his writing would be clearer if he had—but he does talk about that body which the people habitually obey and whose commands bind the Courts, and that body can conveniently be called the legal Sovereign.

Still more confusing is Austin's treatment of the forms which the sovereign body may take (pp. 244 *sqq.*). He considers them purely from the point of view of numbers, according to the proportion the governing body bears to the governed. Government by one is Monarchy. Government by more than one is Aristocracy in a wide generic sense. If the proportion of governing to governed is small, this is Oligarchy. If it is somewhat larger this is Aristocracy in a strict sense. If it is very large, this is Democracy. This is no doubt derived from Aristotle, but it differs widely from its original, an account of which can be seen in Sidgwick (*op. cit.* p. 579). Aristotle does not deal with numbers alone: other factors come into account, especially the aims of the governing body. For him a government of one may be a Monarchy or a Tyranny, the distinction turning partly on the circumstances of its creation, but mainly on the manner of government, the aims of the Sovereign. Austin's analysis has nothing directly to do with the aims of government and he adopts only so much of the Aristotelian scheme as is relevant to his purpose. But Aristotle has one important point in common with Austin, at least with Austin at this point. He knows nothing of any distinction between the political and the legal Sovereign. He could not; in his time it did not exist. It results from the much later invention of representative government. For Austin to ignore it, as he here does, is a blunder. The classification by numbers can hardly be said to have any meaning as applied to the legal Sovereign. The British Parliament is about a thousand 'commanding' many millions. It is therefore an oligarchy and the same is true of nearly all modern States which are not monarchies in effect. The classification is of no value save as applied to the political Sovereign, and under modern conditions it is of little use even in that case. In a small city State or a canton of Switzerland the machinery can be, and is, simple, but in larger States there is a division of function and responsibility which makes the numerical test very uninstructive. Any two States with a similar electoral franchise would be classed together under this scheme, though in reality they might be widely different. The franchise in the German Republic under the Weimar Constitution was very wide, like ours, but the restrictions on the legislature, and the wide powers of the president, made the system very different from ours. The same is true of the Constitution of the United States, with its complex checks and powers. So various are the forms of distribution that it may be doubted whether any classification has much value. The various groupings and distinctions to be found in modern treatises are, by reason of the diverse distributions of function, very complex and those in books with a claim to be philosophic are still more complicated. Political philosophers, under the commanding influence of Aristotle, deal in the same treatise with the nature of the actual State, and with the ideal State, the aims which, in the writer's view, the framers and manipulators of governments ought to have in mind. In the hands of Aristotle this creates little difficulty; the problems are relatively simple. But in dealing with modern conditions this fusion leads to confusion of language if not of thought.

All the discussion in the preceding pages has been concerned with the notion 'law', with what Austin called 'Positive Law'. It was long ago observed that the word 'Positive' serves little purpose. There seem to be other objections to it, as Austin uses it. One may use a term in any sense one will, provided one uses it always in the same sense. Austin makes considerable use of the right, but is not very careful of the proviso. He uses 'Positive' in two senses, neither being its ordinary grammatical sense. In the expression 'Positive Law', as 'law' implies for him 'general command', 'Positive' must mean 'set by political superior'. In the expression 'positive morality', as 'morality' contains the notion 'non-political', 'positive' must mean 'set by human authority'. He uses 'superior' consistently, but in a very distinctive sense; it means 'stronger', able, if need be, to inflict evil. There is nothing of what we commonly call 'moral' about this superior, any more than there is in the word 'moral' as used by him. He shews (pp. 174 *sqq.*) that, for him, a rule set by a non-political superior is 'positive morality' whether it be good or evil. A moral rule is one which you can be compelled by a non-political superior to obey. If you tell a boy that you will thrash him if he does not torment a smaller boy, he is, for Austin, under a moral duty to do it. If another tells him he will thrash him if he does, he is under two conflicting duties, both, for Austin, moral duties. There are thus many moralities, that of the man commanding, that of any other person or persons, that of the community, that which you think the community ought to hold, that which other people think the community ought to hold, and that which, in fact, the community ought to hold. All are equally 'morality' for Austin. And, as we shall see, the same non-ethical quality attaches to his 'right' and 'duty' (*post*, p. 109). He would no doubt have rejected the 'right divine of kings to govern wrong', but he could not consistently have objected to the proposition that there may be a right or duty to do wrong. He seems hardly conscious of the difficulties resulting from his use of the word 'morality'. He says, consistently, that morality can conflict with Divine Law, but clearly this must mean the morality of someone other than the speaker. Austin could hardly say, 'the Deity regards this conduct as wrong, but I am of a different opinion'.

We have assumed that while the legislature in this country is the legal Sovereign, the electorate is the political Sovereign, the body in which, with us, political power finally rests. It is paralysed while there is a Parliament. Strictly we may say that Jurisprudence is not concerned with the political Sovereign; it deals only with the commands which bind the Courts and the source of those commands. But the matter is handled in some modern books on Jurisprudence, and as some writers have held that what we have called the legal Sovereign is not the commander of the law, it may be well to consider the alternatives offered and, in that connection, to examine for a moment what has been said as to the identity of the political Sovereign.

The main consideration which has prevented many writers from accepting the legislature as the legal Sovereign, as the real commander, is the fact that there are communities in which that body cannot make what laws it likes. If the State can, as it sometimes does, so organise itself, or be so organised, as to limit the powers of the legislature, then it is difficult to treat the legislature, whether in the actual case it is so limited or not, as really supreme. Consequently it is thought of as an 'organ' of something else. What is that something else? It is not the electorate, for the same reason; there are in some communities things which the electorate cannot authorise the legislature to do. It must then be something wider than the electorate. It is easy to fall back on the State, but we have already seen how vague and elusive this conception is. Can we say that it is the organ of society, i.e. of everybody in the community? But this 'society' is an entirely extra-political conception. Moreover, when the society has got itself formed into a State, it no longer has any powers; it is the Frankenstein of a very powerful monster. It can affect the State only by way of revolution, which is negation of a polity. It seems absurd to say that the legislature is the organ of something which has no control over it. No doubt the legislature will commonly try to meet the wishes of the people; a good citizen tries to meet the wishes of his neighbours, but he is not an organ of them.

The whole difficulty rests on the assumption that there must be in every polity some unfettered legislative authority. This is not an axiom. It is not a proposition obviously true, self-evident; it needs proof and this cannot be provided. In fact, it is not true. A political society may very well by reason of its historical development be so constituted that, while it is independent of outside authority, it has within its organisation no power that is not somehow limited. This seems to be the condition of the United

States. It is impossible to apply the Austinian conception to this state of things. Where the legislature is unfettered, it is the Austinian, the legal, Sovereign, since the Courts cannot consider any remoter authority when the will of the legislature is clear. That is what 'Sovereign' means for Austin; whether it is a convenient use of the word is immaterial. There may be all sorts of intermediate positions, e.g. one body may have the power of legislation subject to the veto of the other. Or the field of legislation may be divided between two bodies. Or there may be a body with only intermittent existence, called into being by some special machinery and having then the power of legislation. In all such cases it may be possible to find the Austinian Sovereign. But what is to be said where there is no such complication, but the thing simply cannot be done? The fetter is imposed by an instrument made under such historical conditions that it gives no means for its amendment in this respect. It has, I think, been said that in such a case the sovereignty is in the document. But this is mere fiction; the document cannot command or alter itself. The real fact is that there is here no Austinian Sovereign.

X

Some Legal Concepts

(a) SANCTIONS

W E have seen that for most writers law is a command or the like and is based on sanctions. To some, indeed, this seems an outworn notion, indeed all those who have convinced themselves that law rests on the 'general will' are some way upon the road to considering sanctions to be a superfluity. But such a view is in contradiction to facts which are within the knowledge of everybody. We have seen (*ante*, pp. 33, 56) that Vinogradoff argues strongly for the view that compulsion and sanction are not essential to the notion of law. But the question is not whether it is a necessary element in law, but whether it is an ever-present factor in law as it is here and now. We may remember that, having satisfied himself that it is not necessary, he rounds off his discussion of the nature of law by a definition which makes it 'enforced or imposed by authority' and that he describes international law as imperfect precisely because it has no specific sanctions. He was as far from the view that our western law does not involve compulsion as he was from the other error, that the reason why the ordinary man obeys the law is the existence of sanctions, which he fears. Taken literally, Vinogradoff may be said to contradict himself, but in fact he is envisaging two states of fact, things as they are and things as, in his view, they might well be. We shall assume in the discussion of sanctions that, at the present time, and not only in England, but everywhere, the law is in fact based on sanctions.

Acceptance of that principle leaves open a number of difficult questions. Can there be a sanction by reward as well as by punishment? There is certainly no inherent impossibility in the notion of a community which induces the people to obey its orders only by a system of rewards. There is at least one case in which our law actually does this. Some forms of disease must be notified to the local authority under penalties, but the State provides a small payment to the doctor who himself notifies. In a purely socialistic régime all supplies might be subject to obedience to law and no other sanction be needed. Austin rejects this. He says that we do not habitually speak of command when we offer a reward; it is breaking with the usual habits of speech. Though, in his mouth, this is Satan reproving sin, there is something in it; no community does so enforce its laws. When it does we may have to revise the definition. But hardly; the refusal of a good which would otherwise be received is an evil. Factory rules are often enforced by fines and there is no difficulty in seeing punishment in a deduction from wages. Jenks (*The New Jurisprudence*, ch. vi) sees the development of sanction by reward as not only possible but desirable.

Bentham (*Principles of Legislation*, ch. vii) admits reward and uses 'sanction' in a very wide sense. Besides divine, moral and legal sanctions, he admits physical sanctions, by which he means the evils or benefits which may be expected to result from action in the ordinary way. Who sits about in wet clothes catches cold. Eat and drink wholesome food in proper quantities and you may expect your body to serve you well. Austin (pp. 93 *sqq.*) answers that this is to dissociate sanction from command altogether, confusing sanction and motive. If two words have each a precise sense the one including the other, as sanctions are a class of motives, to confuse them is to impoverish the language. But in fact motives operate and can be said to exist only if we are aware of them, but these physical sanctions operate whether or no, so that regarded as commands they are sanctions. Bentham did not regard them as commands, and dissociates sanction and command. But if they are commands, they are divine commands and he already has these. Physical sanctions would be a sub-head. Divine sanctions would be of two kinds, those operating here and now and those of the next world. In fact the classification distinguishes them by their character and not as it does the others, moral, legal, divine, by their sources.

A more puzzling case is that of sanction by nullities, which is prominent in discussions of Jurisprudence. The case to which it is most commonly applied is to rules such as that of our law that a will must have two witnesses. This, it is said, is a command sanctioned by nullity. But if we take this view we soon get into difficulties. If there is a sanction, there is a duty and a right. Who has the right? On whom is the duty? There can be no duty on the beneficiary, who commonly knows nothing of the matter. There can be none on the person entitled on intestacy; he hopes no doubt that there will be no witnesses. The duty then must be on the testator. But there can be no right in either the beneficiary or the successor *ab intestato*, who certainly does not want the witnesses. The right too, it seems, must be in the testator, which is absurd. Perhaps we may say the right is in the State. The testator is under a duty to the State to have his will witnessed, a conditional duty—he need not make a will, but if he does it must be attested. But the same analysis should apply to the rule that a gratuitous promise is void unless it is under seal. Here the duty cannot be on the maker; he can hardly be said to be under the penalty of not being liable. It must then be on the beneficiary. But there is no logical reason for differentiating between the two cases, and a duty in the beneficiary under the will we saw to be impossible. In neither case can he control the matter. He is like a person who has acquired a potential right on a condition beyond his control. There are many such cases. It will not do to say that the testator has a right to have two witnesses. He has, and persons who prevent him may be liable. But that is not sanction by nullity. The whole contention seems to be an artificial solution of a problem which does not really exist. The truth seems to be that this provision is not a command at all. Though a statute is a command, it does not follow that every sentence in it is. It may be part of a command. Kelsen (*Law and Peace in Inter-*

national Relations, pp. 18, 19) observes, of constitutional rules which have no sanction, that they are incomplete legal norms, 'norms by which an element is determined which is common to all legal norms providing sanctions, the provision regarding the procedure by which this norm must have originated in order to be applied as a valid norm'. That is, it is not a norm but part of a norm. In particular it may be definition, as it is here, though it be couched in imperative form.[1] What it comes to is a rule that the disposition of a man's property by his will is binding, and a will is a document executed in a certain way. The same is true of many procedural rules. A man need not enforce his rights, but, if he wants to do so, he 'must' take certain steps. If I want to speak to a man on the telephone I 'must' call him up. There is no sense in saying that I am under a duty to call him up, yet this follows from acceptance of the illustration of sanction by nullity which we have been discussing. A *sine qua non* is not an imperative.

Other cases look more plausible. If a contract is induced by fraud, the innocent party has a choice; he may claim to have the contract set aside or enforce it claiming damages for the fraud. Here we may perhaps say that nullification is a sanction, not nullity, as, so far as third parties are concerned, the contract is operative till set aside. But there is in any case an action for damages and the right to set aside is only an addition to the sanction. Misrepresentation gives a sharper case. If a contract is induced by innocent misrepresentation, not amounting to a promise, the injured party may set the contract aside, but has no other remedy—sanction by nullification. The right of the party misled to treat the contract as valid or to nullify it is a real sanction, not by nullity; the discretionary right is valuable. The unwitnessed will is void; there is no discretion about the matter.

An agreement may be void by reason of certain forms of mistake. Is this sanction by nullity? It might be said that, as the error is not due to negligence or imputable ignorance or

1 See e.g., Eastwood and Keeton, *The Austinian Theories*, p. 21.

any misconduct, it is absurd to talk of breach of duty. But the law might well have a rule making one party an insurer against error in the other, at least to this extent. But, in fact, here too it is matter of definition. A binding agreement requires, *inter alia*, mutual assent. Of this the terms of the 'agreement' are the best evidence, and it is usually held that the law is not concerned with states of mind except as evidenced, and the mistake must be proved by external evidence. But, apart from that, contract requires consent and where fundamental error exists there is no consent and therefore no contract. It is again definition, having nothing to do with sanction by nullity. A plausible case is that of bets, which the Courts will not enforce, but do not otherwise penalise. But even here, if we begin, as most of our books on contract do, by defining contract as agreement enforceable at law, and then state a rule that bets will not be enforced, a bet is not within the definition of a contract. It is much on the level of an informal agreement without consideration, so that here too the conception of sanction by nullity is not necessary. But it may perhaps be admitted that to say there is a rule against betting, sanctioned by nullity, is the most obvious way of looking at the matter, though it seems to be rather popular than exact. Altogether the notion of sanction by nullity does not seem very valuable.

(b) RIGHTS, LIBERTIES, ETC.

No word in the law has been so much discussed as 'right'. It is not easy to define, but the most accepted definition seems to be 'an interest or an expectation guaranteed by law'. Most writers base their treatment on rights. Hearn, however (*op. cit.*), bases his treatment on duties, partly it seems from the idea that, in good taste, duties should come first and partly because duties cover the ground and rights do not, as, in his view, the State can be subject to duties but cannot have rights. And there are writers, not exactly on Jurisprudence *stricto sensu*, but on politics, who deny that there are such things as rights; for them there are only duties. Professor Laski, in one of the few criticisms he allows himself on his leader Duguit, justly observes that even this involves rights, for one must at least have the right not to be impeded in carrying out one's duty (*Law in the Modern State*, p. xxvii). But as these writers, notwithstanding their legalistic language, are really discussing political science, not law, and, in fact, not what is, but what ought to be, their views are not here material.

A right, as above defined, includes interests and expectancies of many kinds, and these have been analysed and placed under separate headings. There are rights *stricto sensu*, privileges, liberties, immunities, powers and so forth. This analysis was most carefully effected by Professor Hohfeld. The distinctions are real, but it is perhaps possible to overestimate their importance; in any case the analysis does not justify some modern utterances. Salmond defines liberties (*op. cit.* § 75) as 'the things which I may do without being prevented by law', and gives as illustration the right to do as I please with my own. Brown (*op. cit.* p. 180) quotes from Austin the correct statement that when we speak of liberties we are primarily thinking of absence of restraint: this is the denotation; protection is the connotation. When we speak of rights this is reversed. But Brown adds, 'strictly we ought not to say that a man has a right to get up at 6 o'clock; what we really mean is that he is at liberty to rise at that hour'. That is a different proposition. What Austin points out is only a difference in point of view from which what are in fact rights can be regarded. That is not to say that when we look at them from the other point of view they are not rights. 'We are not', says Brown, 'thinking of duties on the part of other citizens not to interfere with him.' That is true, but that is not to say that the duty is not there. They are rights, as indeed Salmond admits, though for the moment we are not thinking of them as such. It would be imprudent to ignore the difference between a lion and a domestic puss, but they are both cats, and liberties are rights, so far as they are protected. Thus writers who expound this doctrine seek for cases in which we can say that a man has liberty to do such and such a thing, but his liberty is not protected. Brown's illustrations are not happy. We need not consider the case he puts of a community which has no laws except against polygamy and smoking—we are concerned with communities which have laws. It is, however, significant that he has to go so far afield for his illustration. But he says also, 'a man is at liberty to make a fool of himself, rather than has a right to do so', and illustrates this by the silly amateur actor, and says that a friend who relieves him from his predicament by diverting the attention of onlookers has infringed no right of his. That is true, but not to the point. If the friend had prevented him by force from acting, he would have infringed a right. All rights are limited by the rights of others. The friend has a right to talk to others, and the actor has no right to their attention. Brown (*loc. cit.*) also deals with the case of the 'right' to make (or, presumably, to receive) a gift. But he says, 'if the paramount idea be that of the obligation upon other citizens not to interfere with him in the exercise of this privilege, we may use the term "right". But if, as is more likely, the paramount idea be that the privilege to make gifts is part of that sphere of activity within which a man is free from external interference or control, we should use the term "liberty".' That is no doubt sound, but the reference to interference shews that it is after all a right with corresponding duties, and why one point of view should be 'paramount' it is not easy to see. Salmond's illustrations are no better. He says an alien has a right, i.e. a liberty, to enter the country, but the government has an equal right to exclude him. That is true, but not to the point. If I prevent an alien from landing when the government has licensed him to enter, I shall be liable to an action. If the government has not licensed him to enter, he has not the liberty. Salmond says that if I have a licence to go on your land, I have no right in the sense in which a right in me is correlative to a duty in you. This seems confused thinking. You may in such a case revoke the licence, but if, I having exercised it before any revocation, you bring an action of trespass against me, you will lose. And if a third party drives me out, I shall have my remedy. My right is protected so long as it lasts. His illustrations about my right to destroy my property and my not having a right to commit theft are incorrect. He says, 'that I have a right to destroy my property does not mean that it is wrong for other persons to prevent me; it means that it is not wrong for me so to deal with that which is my own'. It must first be noted that the question is not whether it is wrong, which is a moral question, but whether it is a wrong, which is a legal question. You may be morally justified in stopping me, but in many cases you will be committing a trespass. You may not be; all rights are limited by the rights of others, and it is easy to see circumstances in which, acting quite within your rights, you will be able to stop me. The whole argument seems to shew a confusion of thought, expressed in the words quoted above, 'correlative to a duty in you'. This assumes that, if there is anyone against whom the right does not avail, there is no right. The real question is: Is there any one against whom it is protected? There is, in all his illustrations. All this is not intended to mean that the distinction is not important; a sound analysis should take account of it, as Austin does. His seems the better way.

It is to be noted that Brown introduces his observations as to liberties into his discussion of liberty. This method does not make for clearness. Liberty (whatever it may mean) is a political conception. Liberties are a legal conception, and it is with legal conceptions alone that analytical Jurisprudence is concerned.

'Liberties' seem to mean our freedom to do as we will with our 'selves' and our property. 'Powers' are on a rather different footing. They need have no connection with any property right in the holder of the power. I may have a power of appointment or even a power of sale over property in which I have no estate, legal or equitable. But Salmond's distinction (*op. cit.* § 76) between these and rights *stricto sensu* does not seem acceptable. He says that of all such things the characteristic mark is that they have no duties corresponding to them. 'My right to make a will corresponds to no duty in anyone else.' In its primary sense this is incorrect. The Roman Law had express provisions dealing with the matter (D. 29. 6; C. 6. 34), and even in absence of such provisions, interference with liberty of action will commonly be a trespass. But Salmond is not thinking of the right to cover a paper with writing, but with the power, by writing, to alter the devolution of property—to make an effective disposition. But when it is so stated it becomes clear that there is no difference between alienation by will and any other alienation, so that the question is whether an owner's right of alienation is a power in this sense, i.e. is there no duty corresponding to it? In one sense, there is. The act here meant is not properly described as making a conveyance, but as giving property to someone, and this 'transitory' instrument creates a right and imposes on everyone a duty not to interfere with the right created. But that is not to the point; it is not a right in the transferor but in the beneficiary. A right under the transfer is not a right to make the transfer. This, however, is not the best way in which to state the matter. All rights are rights to act or to abstain, not to produce legal effects. To say that he has a right that his act shall produce that effect is to imply that if he liked it would not have that effect, and this is not true. The act will produce the legal effect whether he wishes it or not. If I own a jug of water I have a right to upset it, but it is absurd to say that I have a right that the water shall fall out. It will do that whether I want it to do so or not. So that, in our case, what I have a right to do is to make the document and this right is protected like any other right. Not every interference with my act will be actionable, for all rights are limited by those of other people. But many will be actionable wrongs.

(c) PRIMARY AND SECONDARY RIGHTS

A familiar classification of rights is into primary and sanctioning or secondary rights. Austin calls the first class 'sanctioned', an ill-chosen name since all rights are sanctioned. Primary rights are those which do not presuppose a wrong done or a maladjustment of property relations which needs adjustment. The other class does in general presuppose a wrong, e.g. a claim for trespass or for breach of contract. Most definitions of right make, as we have seen, a definite reference to enforcement. It is possible to argue that primary rights are not within this definition, for enforcement implies, in general, a wrong done. A right of property cannot come into Court till there is interference, a right of contract till there is a real or alleged breach of it. This proposition, however, is in fact far from true. The Roman *praeiudicia*, the German *Feststellungsklagen* and our own 'originating summonses' bring primary rights into Court—no right need have yet been infringed. It is perhaps only in our own law and in relation to contract that it can even look like a truth. However, it is contended that so-called primary rights are not rights at all, but merely states of fact, the existence of which is the condition on which, in some event, a right may arise to which law will give protection. In support of this it is pointed out that you may be said to have no right to performance of a contract, but only to money compensation if it is not performed; specific performance is exceptional and often impossible. This view was expressed by Mr Justice Holmes in his *Common Law* (p. 300), and it recurs in the Pollock-Holmes correspondence, from a number of passages in which we can see Holmes' view in more detail (see I, 21, 119, 177; II, 55, 200, 234).[1] His position seems to be that the making of a contract is the taking of a risk; the liability in contract is exactly analogous to that in tort. If you commit a tort, you are liable to pay damages. If you commit a contract, you are liable to pay damages, unless something happens (i.e. performance) over which you may or may not have control. It is a conditional liability to pay damages. There is no reason to speak of promise in the matter at all; in particular, it is not a case of alternative obligation. (This in reply to an objection by Pollock.) To this Pollock makes various objections

1 See Buckland, *Camb. L. J.* VIII, pp. 247 *sqq.*

(see I, 79, 80; II, 201, 234, 235). Such a view he says disappoints reasonable expectations. (You don't buy a right to damages, you buy a horse.[1]) It is inconsistent with the law of specific performance. It is inconsistent with the doctrine that premature refusal to perform is a breach. It is inconsistent with the rules about frustration, and the like. To the 'reasonable expectation' point Holmes answers (II, 55), 'I don't see why the cases on damages do not embody the principle of reasonable expectation: he must know that the person he contracts with believes that he accepts the contract with the special condition attached to it.' That seems to be no answer. He knows indeed that he may be put off with damages, but that is not what in the normal case he either wants or expects. But in any case the objection is not fatal; the law often disappoints reasonable expectations; it did in Sinclair v. Brougham ([1914] A. C. pp. 398 sqq.). As to specific performance, Holmes replies that this is not common law and is exceptional. That again is no answer. Pollock observes that it is the normal remedy in other systems, e.g. German Law.[2] That must mean that our common-law conception of contract is utterly different from that of Germany, which is of course not impossible but certainly has no presumption in its favour. And when the King's Bench Division is trying a case on contract and decides to give specific performance, it is presumably compelled to shift from one conception of contract to an entirely different one. Holmes does not in fact meet the objection. As to the point that if there is no obligation to perform, refusal to do so cannot be a breach, it is no answer to say that the doctrine is wrong, for it is very ancient in the law (Pollock, II, 74). The frustration point Holmes does not seem to touch on. But it is surely worth noting that if this analysis is correct no unilateral

1 Cf. D. 18. 4. 21 (Paul), 'tibi enim rem debebam, non actionem'.

2 He asks where they got it, not from Classical Roman Law. Of course not; they did not deal in classical law. They got it from the Pandectists who got it from the Corpus Iuris Civilis. The point is that, as the context shews, Pollock would like to find a Germanic origin for it.

agreement could ever be void for frustration or impossibility initial or supervening. For the only obligation is to pay damages, and our law, like the Roman, takes the optimistic view that it is never impossible to pay money.

There seem to be other odd results of this doctrine. I agree with an artist to paint a picture for me. He states a very high price, to which I agree, say £100. As a matter of fact, such a picture painted by him would never be worth more than £50 in the market. Next day he comes to me and says, 'I am liable to pay you damages if I do not paint the picture. I prefer to pay the damages, which is all I am bound to do. Your damages are £50. Here they are. Now, please pay me the £100, for I have carried out my contract.' No one will suppose that he will get away with it, but it is difficult to see why he should not, on this analysis.

Holmes' neat parallel, 'commit a tort, commit a contract', is misleading. A man who has committed a tort has rendered himself liable to proceedings. That is what the word, in this connection, means. It comes from the Latin, no doubt through the Roman Law, and *commissum* is an actionable wrong done. But one who 'commits' a contract in Holmes' sense, i.e. makes one, has not rendered himself liable to proceedings, though later events may have this effect. He has done no wrong and the word 'commit' is quite inappropriate. A man 'commits' a contract not when he makes it, but when he breaks it. The Roman texts bring this out clearly. Where we say that a man has committed a breach of his contract, they say what can be rendered as 'he has committed his contract', or 'his contract is committed.' Thus in D. 45. 1. 63; 46. 2. 14. 1, where the money is immediately recoverable under a promise, the *stipulatio* is committed. In D. 35. 1. 67, in similar circumstances, *committitur stipulatio*. In D. 2. 11. 13; 39.1. 13. 1, where the money is not immediately recoverable under the promise, *stipulatio non committitur*. There are many other texts of the same sort. This meaning is not of course confined to *stipulatio*. If any term (*lex*) of an agreement is

broken it is *commissa* (D. 18. 3. 4. 2). If an enactment is disobeyed, it is 'committed' (D. 37. 4. 10. 4, '*si per alios committitur
edictum*'). And the *dies committendi* is the day of the breach
(D. 4. 4. 38 *pr.*). Thus Holmes' analogy, tempting as it looks, is
unconvincing.

We may leave to others the question whether the conception
can be fitted to our old and modern systems of pleading. It is
certain that it could not be applied in Roman actions. In the
legis actio in personam the plaintiff declares that something is due,
namely what was promised, and the defendant denies this. If
what was due was not what was promised, but damages, the
defendant must always win. So in the later formulary system,
an action, on a promise of a certain thing, expressly made *condemnatio* depend on the liability for the thing promised, not
on damages. '*Si paret Nm. Nm. Ao. Ao. tritici Africi optimi modios
centum dare oportere*' (Lenel, E.P. (3), 240). If the only obligation
were to pay damages, this claim must fail. It must be remembered
that this was at a time when the judgement was necessarily for
money, and specific performance had not even the limited scope
which we allow it.

For Holmes what the *promissor* is bound to do is to pay damages,
but the liability is avoided if something else happens (what is
commonly called performance of the contract). The Romans
had a convenient terminology for this state of things. What you
are bound to do is *in obligatione*; the thing by which the liability
can be avoided is *in solutione*, a *facultas*. The common cases are
noxal surrender of a slave who has committed a delict, which is
a *facultas* and way of avoiding payment of damages, while the
action is pending, or before, in classical and later law (D. 5. 3. 20. 5;
42. 1. 6. 1), and the case where a man takes a promise to pay to
him or a third party; payment to the third party is a *facultas*,
in solutione (Inst. 3. 19. 4; D. 45. 1. 56. 2; 46. 1. 16 *pr.*; *h.t.* 23;
46. 3. 95. 5; *h.t.* 98. 5; *h.t.* 98. 6). The material point of this distinction is that, if circumstances destroy the obligation, the *facultas*
no longer has any significance, but facts annulling the possibility

of the *facultas* have no effect whatever on what is *in obligatione* (D. 44. 7. 44. 5). If, under Roman Law, *A* promised by *stipulatio* to give *B* a horse, this was a binding contract. If now the horse was killed by pure accident after the promise but before delivery, then, according to Holmes' theory, since it is the damages which are *in obligatione* and the horse is only *in solutione,* the destruction of the horse ought to produce no effect at all on the obligation. *A* must still pay *B* the value of the horse. But that was not the law. The accidental destruction of the thing promised released the *promissor* (D. 45 I. 23, 33, etc.).

Thus it does not seem possible to square Holmes' doctrine either with English Law or with Roman Law. It is surely permissible to think that a conception which is inconsistent with both the great systems of law which divide the western world is of no great value in Jurisprudence. It may be true, as Pollock says (II, 201), in some other planet. It may even be true in old Chinese Law, for we are accustomed to find, in China, reversals of our European notions. It might be a profitable factor in discussions *de lege ferenda* or in discussions of abstract law of the Kantian or Hegelian types. But as an element in the analysis of law as it actually is, it seems to be useless.

These various notions, that there are no rights but claims, and therefore no *iura in rem*, that since what the judge says is law, there is no law and no right under it, till a Court has passed upon it, that for the same reason, a statute is not law till the Court has interpreted it, all these seem to be pretty much on a par with a child's view of the electric light. The child, observing that, within his experience, the existence of a light depended entirely on the question whether the switch was on or off, came to the erroneous conclusion that the switch was all there was to it, ignoring altogether the organisation behind the switch and the fact that the switch is merely a device by means of which the operation of this institution or organisation behind the switch is controlled. The judge too is merely a device, to control the working of the institution which we call the law. Except in cases where there was no law and he has to legislate, he no more makes the law (or at least has no more business to make it, for he may be wrong) than the switch makes the light or the organ blower makes the music. The judge is a concession to the limitations of the human intellect. It is one of the very many cases (one who has not reflected on this matter will be surprised on finding how numerous they are) in which the matter is referred to somebody's decision, because we have no better means of arriving at the truth. Where a man owns a house he has what we call the right of property, really a complex of rights. He is, in relation to that house, in a position in which no one else is. If someone interferes with his enjoyment it has to be determined whether the interference is an infringement of his 'rights'. That cannot be left to the parties. If he wants to raise the point, he is compelled by the State to refer it to the arbitrament of a judge, who has to turn out the legal result much as a calculating machine turns out the result of complex numerical data. No doubt he is not so nearly infallible as the machine, but he is the best we can do, better at any rate than the ordeal or compurgation which he has replaced or even than Judge Bridlegoose. But he is only a device, operating on certain data (in his case, the facts and what we call the law), and the data were in existence before the judge, or the machine, got to work on them. The judge, in deciding a case, except where there is no principle which governs it, or there are competing principles, acts, or is expected to act, on certain principles which existed before he set to work. So too the statute is there and is one of the data for the judge, before he gets to work. It is absurd to say that a statute which has never been disobeyed is not law. The fact that a judge may go wrong is a defect in the device; it is not his essential function, as these theories seem to make it.

Holmes' doctrine is in one way different from those others with which it may be associated. If he is right, some hitherto accepted rules of law are wrong. But the other theories do not seem intended to lead to this result. They are attempts to construct an exact and convenient terminology. And the word 'right' is certainly very hard worked in our books. Exactitude is perhaps hardly in question, for we can call a phenomenon what we like. The new terminology does not seem more convenient. When a man makes a contract he acquires or confers, or both, something. The economic situation is changed in a way of which the law will take account. A party has acquired what we have been in the habit of calling a right, what the Romans called a *res*. Is there any advantage in calling it a state of facts to which the law, in certain events, will attach a right? Acquisition of a right is simple, but acquisition of a state of facts is not very intelligible. 'Potential rights' is more intelligible, but not satisfactory, for, if certain events happened, say, Acts of Parliament, I might have all sorts of rights which I now have not. If we say it is a conditional right, arising if the promise is broken, this will not fit Roman Law, for if the rights under a contract of sale are conditional the risks do not pass (D. 18. 6. 8 *pr.*); on a straightforward sale they do. How the matter would stand in English Law I do not know. Using traditional language we should say that an agreement to sell specific goods in a deliverable state transfers ownership. Whether it is more helpful to say that the transaction creates a state of facts in which the buyer will have certain rights if anyone takes or meddles with or culpably damages the thing, may be doubted. There is something to be said for the expressions 'primary' and 'secondary', though they are nowadays unfashionable. Holmes' doctrine follows necessarily from the proposition that there are no rights but rights of action. If that proposition leads to impossible consequences, it seems that it must be wrong. For though the law is not necessarily logical in all its details, the principles of Jurisprudence ought to be.

In considering the cogency of the view that all a man can be entitled to claim is money compensation, it must be remembered that for tort or delict damages are normally the only conceivable remedy. You cannot uncommit the trespass, and so soon as you

have passed beyond the notion of *talio* there is nothing for it
but a money *solatium*. And *assumpsit*, the basis of our modern
law of contract, was originally an action in tort. So, in Roman
Law, non-return of a thing lent or deposited was originally not
thought of in contractual terms, but as a piece of dishonesty.
The earliest contract which was perhaps without these associa-
tions is *stipulatio*, and this was at first always a promise of money,
so that a condemnation for money would lead to actual performance. It must also be remembered that many of the actions
which we think of as contractual, and which were contractual
in later law, were originally penal, i.e., police measures. It is not
therefore surprising that *condemnatio* in money characterises both
systems. But where it obviously would not serve the Roman
Law very early found a way out. In those cases of *fiducia* where
breach of the *fiducia* involved an evil which money could not
set right, e.g. in *emancipatio* or *adoptio*, the actual carrying out
of the undertaking seems to have been enforced by the magistrate.
In real actions and some others the *iudex* had authority to order
actual restitution instead of money compensation, though here,
if the defendant was recalcitrant, it came to a money payment
in the end. And in the later Roman Law it was recognised that
money compensation was not always a proper way of dealing
with the case, and specific performance could always be obtained
if it was possible. Then at least it was clear that the plaintiff's
right was to actual satisfaction of the undertaking.

The root idea underlying this modern notion seems to be that
every right is a claim, that the idea 'right' imports a ground of
complaint against someone. From this it is a natural corollary
that there is no such thing as a right *in rem*. Any claim under
such a right must, it is said, be a claim against an individual. The
right is thus no more than a set of potential rights *in personam*.
The so-called right of property, with its almost infinite content,
is no more than potential rights of action for trespass or nuisance.
Such a right, it seems, is 'in the air' until someone attacks it by
doing something that gives a right of action. In fact the only

solid ground in the legal universe is the floor of a law Court. However, those concerned with the Roman Law or indeed with the history of our own law must make terms with the notion of *ius in rem* or real action, however illogical they may think it. But it is difficult, with the tendency to think of all rights as claims, to accept the notion of *ius in rem* without arriving at claims *in rem*. Windscheid, who seems first to have made the expression '*Anspruch*' fashionable, arrived at what he called a '*dingliche Anspruch*' (*Lehrbuch des Pandektenrechts*, I, § 43), this being, so long as no one has interfered, a claim to forbearances. This does not mean that for him the claim was only to damages; for him, in contract, the claim is to actual performance; in property it is a claim to actual forbearances. His view is inconsistent with the doctrine that a contract right is a right only if there has been a breach, and then only a right to compensation. For, on that view, there is no claim to forbearance, but only a state of facts which will give a claim to damages if the forbearance is not maintained, and a man who has at the moment no rights of action against anyone has no rights at all. He is a rightless man. Whether that is a reasonable doctrine, whether it represents anyone's real view of the legal system, we need not consider. Analytical Jurisprudence is of use only so far as it helps to the comprehension of actual legal systems and it is impossible to understand the Roman procedure or the Roman texts without treating the distinction between rights *in rem* and *in personam* as fundamental. The Romans indeed make the distinction between the remedies and not the rights, but the point is the same and their way of handling it is all the more significant. The plaintiff in a *vindicatio* alleged that he had a *ius in rem*, e.g. ownership, and he had to prove it. The *actio communi dividundo* was *in personam* but, to have a *locus standi* in it, it was necessary to be one of the co-owners. And it involved no wrong done. As a result of historical accident we no longer have in our law real actions in the Roman sense, but we once had them, and even now the machinery of originating summonses and petitions by trustees for instructions, where no wrong has yet been done, seems to imply primary rights *in rem*, i.e., available against persons generally.

Jenks (*The New Jurisprudence*, pp. 172 *sqq.*; see also Hearn, *op. cit.* pp. 53, 54) takes the war into the enemy's country by the criticism that the so-called sanctioning duties are not duties at all, but mere liabilities. A libeller 'is liable to undergo punishment or to pay damages or both, but he is not under a duty to do either, because he has no choice in the matter'. For Jenks the essence of a legal duty is that the sanction of it should be avoidable by obedience to the law. It is difficult to see what answer Austin could have had to this as a criticism of his notion of sanctioning duties, in view of his conception of duty as liability to a sanction on disobedience. Jenks does not apply this point to the matter we are discussing, but his criticism, if well founded, as it seems to be, must lead supporters of the view that the only rights are to the sanctions of the Courts to the paradoxical conclusion that the only rights are those which have no corresponding duties.

The view here combated seems to rest on a misconception of the nature and importance of the sanction. It makes the sanction the focal point of the law while in fact it is only a piece of mechanism which, men being what they are, we cannot do without. If all men were law-abiding and fully informed, there would be no need of sanctions, and law Courts could go out of business. It might be said that there would then be no difference between legal and moral duties, but that is not quite so; there would still be the distinction between those rules which were in some way promulgated by the central authority and those which were not. Where they conflicted the legal duty would be to obey the former. What it is sought here to maintain is that the primary function of the Courts is to determine the facts and the law applicable to them. The sanction is only an incidental and not the central thing.

(d) RIGHTS AND DUTIES IN THE SOVEREIGN

A problem suggested by the conception of the law as command of the Sovereign is the question whether the Sovereign can have legal rights and duties. Some confusion has been caused by using the word 'State', and by bringing into the discussion our maxim 'the king can do no wrong'. But the State is apt to mean the executive—acts of State are ordinarily acts of the executive and that is really what is meant in every-day practice by the maxim that the king can do no wrong (though the rule would cover acts done by him in his private capacity). But the executive is not Sovereign, and there is nothing 'necessary' in our rule—a rule which does not exist in other systems, has exceptions in ours, and is in all probability not destined to much longer life. The real question is: Can the Austinian Sovereign—with us, the king in Parliament—have legal rights and duties? Austin's answer is, for him, very brief. Legal obligation, he says, consists in liability to a sanction. The Sovereign cannot be said to be liable to a sanction which, by his own will, he can put out of action. A duty is imposed by someone and if any one can impose duties on me, I am not, for Austin, Sovereign (*op. cit.* I, pp. 270 *sqq.*). It may be added that Jellinek's 'auto-limitation' is merely a phrase—there is still only voluntary submission, not liability. As to rights, Austin says that every right involves three persons, him who confers it, him on whom it is conferred and him against whom it is effective. In a so-called right of the Sovereign there are only two of these persons, and to say that a Sovereign can give himself a right is to confuse might and right (pp. 290 *sqq.*).

As to duties, this seems sound if the law is a command of the Sovereign, though it has no cogency for those who dispute this analysis. But even those who accept Austin's analysis do not all accept this conclusion. Thus Brown says (*op. cit.* p. 194): 'Sovereignty does not preclude the notion of obligation, but only the notion of limitation by a power external to itself. If a sovereign, having laid down a law that contracts shall be enforced, enters into contracts with its own subjects and if these contracts are enforced as a matter of fact even as against the sovereign, it is impossible to deny that the sovereign is under a legal duty towards its subjects. We cannot refuse to describe the sovereign's liability as a legal duty on the ground that the sanction is self-imposed, if, as a matter of fact, the sanction is invariably admitted by the sovereign and applied by the Courts.' Every phrase of this passage is open to exception. It is an abuse of language to say that there can be obligation in the sense of compulsion, apart from external control. The executive is not the Sovereign, in Austin's sense. Our Sovereign has not 'laid down a law that contracts shall be enforced', but that agreements satisfying certain requirements between persons subject to the law shall be enforced, and this was not by statute but by certain writs, addressed only to subjects. The Crown never admits its liability in tort, so that it picks and chooses, though practice in this matter is likely to alter. The Crown admits claim on contract, as otherwise no one would contract with it. So, in private life, many obligations which could not be enforced are carried out, though there was no legal duty, and a man who pays a claim which he thinks not to be due, to avoid scandal or other inconvenience, is not under a legal duty. But a rival definition of a right creates a difficulty. If we define a right as a reasonable expectation, which the law will recognise, must we not say that one who makes an agreement with the State has, on all the facts, such an expectation, and therefore a right, implying a duty on the other side? But the man who agrees with the State knows that he cannot sue without a fiat and that this can be and sometimes is refused, so that it still seems difficult to think of the position as one of legal duty. But in fact this case we have been discussing has nothing to do with the matter. The Crown is not the Austinian Sovereign. If, as may well happen, a statute is passed making the Crown or a department of State liable for torts committed by its officers, this will impose no duty on the Austinian Sovereign, the supreme legislature, the uncommanded commander. To refute

Austin's contention it would have to be shewn that an action would lie against the Crown in Parliament or the executive, in respect of things done under and within the authority of an Act of Parliament. And no such action would lie.

The case is less clear as to rights. There are in truth three parties, but it is not shewn that two parts cannot be played by the same person. The person who imposes the sanction cannot be the person who endures it, for it cannot affect his action; he need not suffer it. But the person imposing and he who benefits may be the same. He, more than any other, can assert the claim and make it effective. Austin objects that this is to confuse might and right, but this itself is a confusion. In a characteristic passage he says: 'This paradoxical expression' (i.e. that might is right), 'a great favourite with shallow scoffers and buffoons, is either a flat truism affectedly and darkly expressed, or is thoroughly false and absurd' (p. 292). This is the same man who says (p. 91): 'being liable to evil from you if I comply not with a wish which you signify, I am bound or obliged by your command, or I lie under a duty to obey it...command and duty...are correlative terms', and (p. 293), 'a right signifies that which...resides in a determinate party or parties by virtue of a given law, and which avails against a party or parties (or answers to a duty lying in a party or parties), other than the party or parties in whom it resides'. Here right is no more than might, a power to cause infliction of evil if a certain course of action is not followed. He seems to apply, in order to deny the name 'right', just those moral considerations which he elsewhere so carefully excludes. It is strange that the same man should have written both passages in the same book. A proposition is not false because it is a truism darkly expressed. The State is not giving itself more power by giving itself a right; by making an evil conditional on conduct it is turning undefined power into Austinian right. Writ, trial, judgement and execution follow just as if the case was between two private citizens. But here too there may be a confusion between Austin's Sovereign and the executive.

To all this the plain objection has been made that as the Sovereign can do anything there is no point in detaching a bit of this power and calling it a right. But is this conclusive? The transaction between the Sovereign and *X* has set up a new state of things in which there exists something which looks like a right, behaves like a right and is enforced like a right, with no fiction or *als ob*. Is there any point in refusing to call it a right? If we prefer to think of a right as only a name for the 'hypostasis of a prophecy', a reasonable expectation which the Courts will satisfy, the same may be said; the transaction has set up such an expectation.

(e) DUTY TO TAKE CARE[1]

If legal duty means liability to a sanction, there can be no legal duty where there is no means of enforcement of any kind. Some ten years ago the writer, having this in mind, published in the *Law Quarterly Review* (1935, pp. 637 *sqq.*) an article in which the view was maintained that our law of negligence was mis-leadingly stated in the books and in the cases. In particular it was said that the rules that there must be proof of a legal duty to take care, and that this duty must be one to the plaintiff, were *eidola fori* having no real existence and no reason for existence. It was concluded that there was no such thing, in civil, as opposed to criminal, law, as a legal duty to take care and therefore no such duty to the plaintiff. This opinion was induced by a comparison of the Roman way of stating the matter on what is substantially the same tort. The Romans called it *damnum iniuria datum*; the tort is the damage inflicted in a certain way, i.e. carelessly or wilfully. The duty is not to damage; the tort, the infringement of a right, is doing the damage. The distinction is not, in practice, of much importance, because, in fact, the two

1 In his *Essays in Jurisprudence and the Common Law* (pp. 110–150) Professor Goodhart, without reference to this particular point, gives an admirable account and criticism of the puzzles created by our way of looking at the law of negligence.

systems reach practically much the same results. But it was sought in the article to shew that it was not wholly unimportant, and, in any case, it is well to state the law correctly, for, some day, one of those incalculable states of fact may arise in which the distinction will be material in a way which we do not now recognise.

The article does not seem to have convinced many people; indeed, from some comments, it would seem that it was regarded as a piece of perverseness which did not deserve attention. It is respectfully submitted that the perverseness, if any, is not on the side of the writer. No one, so far as the writer has seen, has done the article the compliment of a refutation in print, but discussion with friends has produced a reply which, as it is not *publici iuris*, cannot be fathered on anyone. The argument of the reply is shortly as follows. It is of course possible to define right in such a way as to make it mean merely liability to a sanction, as Austin does, but that is a faulty analysis. The proper analysis is in terms of 'ought'. We cannot keep out the 'ought'. As Kelsen says, law is in the region of *das Sollen*, not in that of *das Sein*. Theoretically therefore a legal duty consists in an 'ought' and thus there is no difficulty in having a legal duty without a sanction. The same conclusion is reached by looking at the cases. A debt unenforceable under the Statute of Frauds may be good consideration for a cheque given in payment of it. A debt barred by the Statute of Limitations may be revived. Though an unregistered dentist cannot sue for work done, he can appropriate a part payment to work done and sue for the value of the materials. There are many other cases of the same kind.

On this there are three things to be said.

i. The fact that 'ought' is essential to law (if indeed it be a fact, as to which something is said below) does not destroy the requirement of sanction. The two requirements are not mutually exclusive. A legal duty with no sanction is, as such, meaningless. It is not distinguishable in practice from a moral duty. So far as it is laid down by authority, if it can be said to be so laid down, it is parallel to those monitions, short of regulation, which have been issued from time to time in the present war, e.g. 'Do not make trunk calls unnecessarily.' These too create no doubt a moral duty, just as there is a moral duty to take care lest you injure other people, but neither of them is a legal duty.

ii. The proposition that we cannot keep 'ought' out of our conception of legal duty seems more than doubtful. No doubt it is true that moral considerations constantly enter into legal discussion. Winfield tells us (*Harv. Law Rev.* 1931, p. 112) that we cannot escape from the moral element in law. When a judge legislates or decides between two analogies, he commonly has moral considerations in view; it is commonly moral considerations which cause him to legislate. But that is not material to the present question, i.e., whether there is such a thing as a legal duty towards X or Y or Z to take care in conduct which may affect him. There is no doubt a moral duty, but it is not a legal duty unless it is sanctioned, enforced, by law. And we have seen that it is not. 'Ought' is an ethical notion and the analysis of a legal notion has nothing to do with its ethical value.[1] Austin's view is correct. 'Legal duty' does not mean that we 'ought' to do the act enjoined on us, but that, if we do not, the law provides the party to whom we owe the duty with means of putting pressure upon us. That is to say, legal duty means simply that we can be made to do the act or, if we do not, to pay a *solatium* to the other party. There are such things (it is enough for the present purpose that there may be) as bad and unjust laws, ordering acts or abstentions which are immoral. We are under a legal duty to obey them. If we say that this imports 'ought', then we 'ought' to act or abstain accordingly. But in cases of this kind, speaking the language of morality, we ought not. Can it be that we both ought and ought not? We can in fact introduce the notion 'ought' to the conception of legal duty only if we give it another meaning, or empty it of all content. The moral

1 So Bergbohm, *Jurisprudenz und Rechtsphilosophie*, cited by Friedmann, *op. cit.* p. 145.

proposition that we ought to obey the law, which most people would accept, has, or may have, its limits (see *ante*, p. 28). There may be laws, there are in Germany at the time of writing, laws which a decent man cannot obey without repulsion. If he obeys them, it is because he fears the legal consequences of disobedience. If you say that he ought to obey them, your 'ought' means only liability to evil if he does not. It is in fact only if a system of law is in accord with a certain philosophy and that philosophy is correct, that we can say, without reserve, that a man ought to obey the law. We are back to the position that an essential of law is the legal imperative, that by this we can identify it, though it commonly has other characteristics. It is difficult to see what the word 'legal' in the expression 'legal duty' can mean, if it does not mean enforceable in some degree by law. A legal duty must be one that has legal effects. No doubt there will be such if damage results to someone from my carelessness, but that is a different matter. The case is comparable to that of a draft agreement. This has no legal effect; it creates no legal rights or duties. If the draft is executed and satisfies other legal requirements, it at once becomes legally enforceable, a contract. The draft without the signature, or the signature without the draft, would have no legal significance. So too the careless conduct without damage, or the damage without anything making it imputable, would have no import at civil law. The breach of duty is the wrongful infliction of damage. And so the Romans put it—*damnum iniuria datum*. What is true of tort in general must be true of the particular case, and Professor Goodhart tells us (*Law Quart. Rev.* 1938, p. 127) that 'for ordinary purposes it is not inaccurate to define a tort as "the breach of a duty not to injure another person"'. The case is analogous to that of Rylands *v.* Fletcher ([1868] L.R. 3 H.L. p. 330). A man who accumulates on his land a quantity of water does so at his peril and is responsible, if not absolutely, at any rate within very wide limits, if the water escapes and does damage. The accumulation of this exceptional mass of water is essential to the tort, but no one will contend that there is a legal duty not to have reservoirs. And it is noticeable that Pollock uses similar language as to our case. He says (*Law of Torts*, ed. 13, p. 451) that 'a man is bound to exercise due care...or, rather, *omits or falls short of it at his peril, namely, of being liable to make good whatever harm may be a proved consequence of the default*'.[1] No doubt he uses the word 'default', but we shall get the same result if we substitute 'conduct' or any other word not implying breach of duty. We are apt to be misled by a very real difference between the two cases. There is nothing contrary to moral duty in having a reservoir. There is, in driving carelessly. But there are countless moral duties which are not legal duties. The difference between the two cases is that in Rylands' case there is at least approximation to liability without fault; in our case there is not. But, for our purpose, that is immaterial.

iii. This leads to the third point, the cases cited to shew that there is a legal duty to take care. There seems to be an underlying idea that enforcement means enforceability by action and nothing else. In support of the proposition that there may be legal duty without enforceability, a number of cases are put in which there is no action but yet there are ways in which the obligation may be made more or less effective. But these cases are not in point. In all of them, whatever their defects, the transaction does produce some legal effects—they are cases of imperfect obligation. The alleged 'duty to take care' is on a different footing. It is not enforceable in any way. If I drive down Piccadilly at sixty miles an hour I am certainly careless, but if I get through without damaging anyone in any way I am under no liability at civil law to anyone. I may be a criminal, but that is another matter—the alleged duty is to some person, not to the State. So far as civil law is concerned my carelessness is without any legal result whatever. On the other hand, in all these cases of imperfect obligation there is a legal duty precisely because there are in all of them ways in which they can be made

1 Italics mine.

more or less effective. In the same way Reinach (*op. cit.* p. 820) says that positive law recognises claims (*Ansprüche*) which are not protected by it, and goes on to give illustrations, similar to those here mentioned. They are all cases in which there is some protection, though it falls short of actionability. There is the same assumption that legal protection and actionability are the same. It was remarked in the writer's earlier article that this duty to take care was a fifth wheel on the coach, that it was not a requirement independent of remoteness but only a case of remoteness. This is confirmed by the language of the judges in dealing with the point. They repeatedly say that there is no duty to X because there was no foreseeable likelihood of harm to him, or the act was not the proximate cause of the damage, with precisely the same conflicts as to the proper formulation as we get in the treatment of remoteness.[1]

1 See the numerous citations in Professor Goodhart's articles (*ante*, p. 110).

Index

OF MODERN AUTHORS CITED

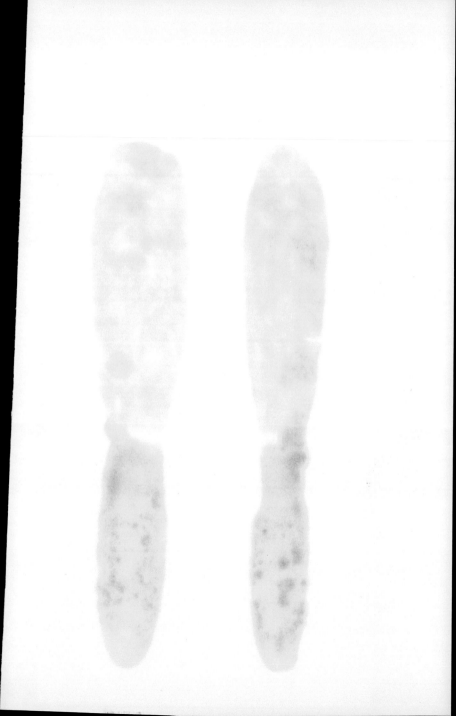

DATE DUE

FEB 22 2016	

GAYLORD   PRINTED IN U.S.A.